"This bold book puts all the main issues on the table. And the main issues are complex and urgent indeed, ranging from whether or in what sense non-Messianic Jews are still in a covenantal relationship with God, to what the Messiah Jesus accomplishes for Jews and Gentiles, to the status of Torah observance in Christian communities, to the significance of the experience of Messianic Jewish synagogues, to the meaning of 'supersessionism' and its relation to the horrific persecution and violence committed against Jews (in the name of Jesus Christ!) by Christians over the centuries. I heartily commend this book as a deeply illuminating and instructive starting point for anyone who wishes to enter into this crucial conversation."

—MATTHEW LEVERING, Mundelein Seminary

"This is an important collection of essays exploring what constitutes a faithful representation of the views and practice of Paul the apostle on the basis of his own testimony in the face of significant pressures in academic circles to affirm a two-covenant theology and make Paul a witness to the same. The principal essayists seek to nurture a response to contemporary Jews that is sensitive to the deplorable history of (Christian) violence and prejudice against them while also not withholding from them that for which Paul passionately prayed—their deliverance in the one Messiah of Jew and Gentile. There is enough here to challenge both those who have espoused the naïve and arrogant supersessionism that Paul opposes in Romans and those who have sought to deny the universal claims Paul makes on behalf of Jesus the Christ and a gospel that is 'for the Jew first and also for the Greek.'"

—DAVID A. DESILVA, Ashland Theological Seminary

"Is supersessionism merely a bully club to hammer those who disagree with orthodox theology? Or is it a theology that misconstrues Paul and has led to the erasure of Jews from the church and the world? Unlike some multi-author volumes discussing important issues, here there is real debate among scholars who differ in substantial ways. Recommended for all who want to know if Jesus and Paul thought God ended his covenant with Jewish Israel and transferred it to the gentile Church."

—GERALD R. MCDERMOTT, author of *Israel Matters* and *Jesus Across the Millennia*

"Mike Bird and Scot McKnight have assembled an outstanding group of scholars to address an important and controversial topic: supersessionism. What I especially appreciate about this book is the care with which this complex concept is defined and contextualized. Readers will come away with a much clearer understanding of what the apostle Paul—himself a devout Jewish follower of Jesus—has to say about historic Israel and its relationship to the church."

—CRAIG A. EVANS, Houston Christian University

GOD'S ISRAEL

AND THE

ISRAEL OF GOD

GOD'S ISRAEL

AND THE

ISRAEL OF GOD

PAUL AND
SUPERSESSIONISM

EDITED BY

MICHAEL F. BIRD
& SCOT MCKNIGHT

LEXHAM
ACADEMIC

God's Israel and the Israel of God: Paul and Supersessionism

Copyright 2023 Michael F. Bird and Scot McKnight

Lexham Academic, an imprint of Lexham Press
1313 Commercial St., Bellingham, WA 98225
LexhamPress.com

Our books are available in print or as digital (Logos) editions in Logos Bible Software.

Print ISBN 9781683596080
Digital ISBN 9781683596097
Library of Congress Control Number 2021948185

Lexham Editorial: Derek Brown, David Bomar, Mandi Newell, Katrina Smith, Jordan Short
Cover Design: Joshua Hunt, Brittany Schrock
Typesetting: Justin Marr, Abigail Stocker

CONTENTS

ABBREVIATIONS

AGAJU	Arbeiten zur Geschichte des Antiken Judentums und des Urchristentums
CD	Cairo Genizah copy of the Damascus Document
Cels.	Origen, *Contra Celsum*
Conf. Ling.	*De confusione linguarum*
CUP	Cambridge University Press
Disc.	*De disciplina christiana*
Ep.	*Epistulae*
Flacc.	*In Flaccum*
Haer.	Irenaeus, *Adversus haereses*
Hist.	Tacitus, *Histories*
HTR	*Harvard Theological Review*
HTS	*Harvard Theological Studies*
Hom. In Rom.	*Homilia in epistulam ad Romanos*
JTS	*Journal of Theological Studies*
Leg.	*Legum allegoriae*
Migr. Abr.	*De migratione Abrahami*
MTSR	*Method and Theory in the Study of Religion*
NICNT	New International Commentary on the New Testament
PP	*Peri Pascha*
Rer. Div. Her.	*Quis rerum divinarum heres sit*
TAPA	*Transactions of the American Philological Association*
War	Josephus, *Jewish Wars*
WUNT	Wissenschaftliche Untersuchungen zum Neuen Testament

CONTRIBUTORS

Michael F. Bird is academic dean and lecturer in theology at Ridley College in Melbourne, Australia.

Ronald Charles is associate professor in the department for the study of religion at the University of Toronto, Canada.

Lynn H. Cohick is provost, dean of academic affairs, and professor of New Testament at Northern Seminary in Lisle, Illinois, United States.

Scot McKnight is professor of New Testament at Northern Seminary in Lisle, Illinois, United States.

Janelle Peters is visiting assistant professor at Loyola Marymount University, California, United States.

David J. Rudolph is director of Messianic Jewish Studies and professor of New Testament and Jewish Studies at The King's University in Southlake, Texas.

Ben Witherington III is professor of New Testament interpretation at Asbury Theological Seminary in Wilmore, Kentucky, United States.

INTRODUCTION TO PAUL AND THE SUPERSESSION CONTROVERSY

MICHAEL F. BIRD

The idea for this book began as a conversation of mutual lament by Scot McKnight and Michael Bird concerning the state of Paul and supersessionism in scholarship. Now "supersessionism" can mean different things to different people, ranging from "the Jews have been replaced by Christian gentiles" through to anyone who finds anything deficient in the Jewish religion that is supplemented by faith in Paul's Christ. We lamented that approaches to supersessionism had been incredibly theologized and even politicized in academia. On the one hand, we recognized that allergies to finding a supersessionism in Paul were often based on legitimate concerns, such as avoiding pernicious perspectives whereby God has replaced ethnic Israel with a gentile church, countering the history of Christian anti-Semitism, discarding cartoonish portrayals of Jews in general and the Pharisees in particular, grounding Paul within his Jewish context, and out of a noble desire to pursue positive interfaith relationships between Jews and Christians. On the other hand, we were exasperated by several things: the weird alliance between secular scholars of religion and dispensational theologians who are dually committed to partitioning first-century Jews from gentile Christianity; Pauline scholars who make Paul sound more like his opponents in Galatia than an apostle to the gentiles who was scourged by synagogue

authorities; the failure to take seriously Paul's christocentric soteriology and critique of Torah-observance; the conundrum of Jewish
Christianity or messianic Judaism if evangelizing Jews is so reprehen-
sible; the inability of scholars to identify the supersessionist aspects of
Qumran and the later rabbis as analogs to Paul; and how the charge of
supersessionism is deployed as a label of derision for anyone who is
not a religious pluralist. As such, we thought it time to have a genuine
conversation about the apostle Paul and supersessionism—the result
of which is this very volume.

The title, *God's Israel and the Israel of God*, takes its cue from a
prominent article by Bruce Longenecker on Paul and supersessionism,[1] and it is intended to presage the question of how ethnic or empirical Israel (i.e., God's Israel) relates to the Pauline churches with their
majority-gentile congregations (i.e., the "Israel of God," to use the
language of Gal 6:16). To that end, Scot McKnight, Michael Bird, and
Ben Witherington provide short essays with their own appraisals of
how the apostle Paul related to the Jewish people in light of his convictions concerning the salvation that God has wrought in the Lord
Jesus Christ. These essays identify a certain degree of supersessionism in Paul as part and parcel of his Christ-centred faith. Thereafter,
four scholars offer their response to the first three essays while also
setting forth their own perspectives concerning how Paul relates his
Christ-faith to his Jewish contemporaries. The conversation partners
include scholars from a diverse range of religious and academic perspectives in order to manufacture a wide-ranging discussion.

Scot McKnight contends that the label of supersessionism amounts
to a bully club in academia used to denigrate non-pluralist schemes
of Christianity. He asserts that supersessionism is intrinsic to any
particularist scheme of Christianity where salvation is attributed to
Christ and to no other. The canonical story, as Christians have tra-
ditionally understood it, maximizes the universal dimensions of the

---

1. Bruce Longenecker, "On Israel's God and God's Israel: Assessing Supersessionism
in Paul," *JTS* 58 (2007): 26–44.

narrative in such a way that it minimizes or deletes the particular dimension of Israel's role in God's plan, and this later aspect is what many find affronting. McKnight finds R. Kendall Soulen's attempts to erase supersessionism in some ways helpful but ultimately unsatisfactory. The upshot would be that the church has no mission to evangelize the Jewish people. McKnight is keen to avoid a replacement of Israel by the church, and he draws on N. T. Wright's work to show that a form of sectarian supersessionism is inevitable in any close reading of Paul's letters, and it does not amount to a "hard" form of supersessionism. Then, taking aims at Mark Kinzer's proposal for a post-missionary messianic Judaism, McKnight argues that Kinzer's proposal of one church for gentiles and another church for Jews is precisely what Paul is arguing against in Galatians. In contrast, he thinks Paul sees the church as Israel-expanded, in which Jewish believers will remain sometimes Torah-observant and gentile believers may not be Torah-observant except in general, but together they will form one fellowship. In the end, McKnight believes it all comes down to the question: Is Jesus Israel's Messiah? If the answer is "yes," then supersession in a salvific sense is unavoidable, with the result that Jesus and the apostles were "supersessionist hermeneuts." The only reason to deny this is to embrace a specifically pluralistic account of salvation, which requires a radical reconfiguration of Pauline thought.

Michael Bird too expresses some frustration with the polemical charge of "supersessionism" that is routinely trotted out in Pauline studies, where its denunciation is tantamount to a type of ritual anathematizing of heretics. Bird argues there are several types of supersessionism; thus, to censure supersessionism as a morally affronting reading of Paul is to assume that all types of supersessionism are the same and they all entail a replacement of Jews by Christians, when they do not. Besides that, Bird points out that supersessionism is ubiquitous in Jewish sectarianism, revolving around which group and which vision for Israel is in a privileged position before God, and forms an intricate part of Paul's own Jewish heritage. Consequently, Bird argues that supersessionism is inescapable in Paul's perspective, given that Paul detects something deficient among his Jewish contemporaries with respect to either the instrument of salvation in Christ or the scope of salvation to include gentiles. Finally, Bird offers a reading of key passages in Paul's letters, principally Romans 9–11, which indicate that in Paul's messianic eschatology Israel is not replaced but expanded to include Christ-believing gentiles within its ranks. According to Bird, Paul uniquely affirms that the distinction between Jews and gentiles is negated in the Messiah even while Paul retains a place for ethnic Israel in God's future purposes. He adds that, even if this approximates to what Paul says, we must still think wisely and responsibly about how to appropriate it for interfaith relations between Jews and Christians.

Ben Witherington contends that a reading of Paul will not countenance the claims made by the Paul-within-Judaism school, which minimizes Paul's contention with his fellow Jews and Jewish Christians. Witherington largely follows the work of John Barclay in arguing that Paul regarded Jewish identity as not negated but transcended by the gospel, and Israel too needed the gift of God offered in Christ. The gospel is for both the Jew and the gentile. Witherington also claims that, in Galatians, Paul is not interested exclusively in the relationship of gentiles to the Jewish law. Paul addresses the attitude (to the law) of Jews like Peter and those for whom ritual impurity was a significant matter. Still, Witherington does not regard the "Israel of God" (Gal 6:16) as a reference to the church; instead, it refers to Jews and perhaps even to the Judaizers. In addition, Witherington's Paul believes Israel has a future when Christ returns, but it will be in Christ—an eschatological future for those currently not in Christ or cut off from the remnant of Jewish Christians. On the crux of supersessionism, he thinks the question is anachronistic and somewhat moot for Paul. Even so, Paul does have a strong conception of the unity of God's people in Christ—Jews and gentiles—and he articulated it in such a way that drew allegations of apostasy. In the end, Witherington avers that for Paul being "in Christ" was where the fulfillment of Israel's future and Israel's mission to be a light to the nations moved forward.

Lynn Cohick supports the three initial essays, sharing with them a common understanding of Pauline supersessionism as a "conviction that Jesus Christ is the fulfillment of the biblical promises of redemption for all people." Cohick believes such arguments can be advanced further by paying attention to Christian "identity" and the relational entailments of being "in Christ." Cohick affirms (with McKnight) that Paul's denial of gentile impurity and relative disinterest in the temple are the true roots of an erasure of differences between Jews and gentiles, but one that was divorced from the story of Israel in the second-century church. Cohick affirms (with Bird) that Christ has agency in Israel's eschatological deliverance, as Jews and Christians share an interlocking destiny. Cohick affirms (with Witherington) that one need not regard an older or lesser covenant as entirely negated or inferior, so the old covenant still retains positive value in Christian theology. Cohick's principal contribution comes by way of some reflections on Melito of Sardis's *Peri Pascha*. She finds in *Peri Pascha* a model of promise and fulfillment so that Christ is the mystery that unlocks God's purposes for his people through several typological presentations detected in the Old Testament. On the positive side, Melito's scheme of fulfillment effectively circumvents Marcionism. Unfortunately, Melito also engages in intensely anti-Jewish polemics by accusing the Jews of deicide (i.e., the murder of God)—an accusation attributable to Melito diverging from the Pauline scheme wherein Israel has stumbled, but not fallen; some branches have been broken off, but they can be regrafted onto the olive tree, the people of God. Cohick concludes that conversations about supersessionism should take account of studies about identity and embodiment as they relate to individual and group relationships. Questions about Paul, Torah, Jews, and gentiles should be framed by stressing identity in Christ, and within that identity an ability to celebrate the distinct tribe, language, and nation of each believer, whether Jewish or gentile.

David Rudolph is a Messianic Jewish scholar, and he pushes back on some of the essays by asking about the covenantal status of non-Messianic Jews. He worries that the views of Bird and McKnight are too similar to N. T. Wright's theology of Israel. The result is that they arguably promote a version of traditional supersessionism character-ized by a third-race theology that envisions Jewish life as obsolete in the new covenant era and the Jewish people as replaced by the church. Such an approach, Rudolph warns, has led to the rise of Christian anti-Semitism and been disastrous for a Christian perspective of the Jewish people. He is particularly concerned about what it means in practice for Jewish-Christian relations and the erasure of Messianic Jews in gentile-dominated ecclesial contexts.

Janelle Peters is a specialist in both ancient Judaism and early Christianity and contributes to the topic from the perspective of the Catholic tradition. She points out that, since the 1960s and the Second Vatican Council, the Roman Catholic church has pivoted in its approach to the Jewish people and its relationship with contemporary Jewish communities. She points out how the 2015 Vatican document *The Gifts and the Calling of God are Irrevocable (Romans 11:29)* intro-duced a new interpretation of Paul's letter to the Romans as acknowl-edging the unceasing validity of the Jewish covenant established by God. Peters in turn briefly examines Paul's image of the grafted olive tree as one drawing on both Jewish and Roman agricultural meta-phors. She believes that Paul emphasizes the value of Jewish heritage in his letter to the Romans on account of his missional coworkers, such as Aquila and Prisca, returning to Rome. Paul, Peters claims, did not cease to be Jewish by his choice to follow Christ, and he and his faith are part of the olive tree's root even as it grows into the gen-tile church. In a similar way, Peters contends that for Paul the gifts of God to the Jews are irrevocable and take the form of church teaching. However, she adds that one must remember that this notion is from a Christian perspective rather than a Jewish perspective. By far, most Jews do not follow Christ and do not derive the essential components of their practice of Judaism from Catholic and Christian teaching in the same way that Christianity bases its self-understanding on the Jewish messiah and the Jewish scriptures. Peters believes that Bird, McKnight, and Witherington have rightly noted how the Jewish sects of the first century grated against one another and could be construed as supersessionist among themselves. Yet modern Judaism does not necessarily agree with one sect over the others, so we must be careful not to claim one sect is closer to contemporary Christianity than it is to contemporary Judaism, particularly in the case of Qumran.

Ronald Charles offers much critical pushback on the three opening essays. Against McKnight, Charles wonders if McKnight's essay is really a proxy war against religious pluralism, and he chides McKnight for assuming that the Bible has one "narratival" view about anything, including the Jews. Charles is perplexed at the commendation of N. T. Wright and the dismissals of R. Kendall Soulen and Mark Kinzer, as this trades in presuppositions rather than actual argumentation. Charles is unpersuaded by McKnight's claim that Paul's "Israel" is "expanded" to include gentiles, if Jews must believe in Jesus in order to be included with this "Israel." Against Bird, Charles questions whether Paul's "messianic eschatology" (Bird's term) really necessitates the kind of supersessionism of which Bird thinks it does. Charles also wonders whether Bird is avoiding the underlying issue: How does he know Paul was right about the Jews being in the wrong? In addition, Bird's essay needs more attention to the sociology of Paul and is perhaps too indebted to the sociology of Pauline scholarship, with its own intrafactional rivalries. Shifting to the core issue, Charles contests Bird's primary thesis: that Paul's Jewish context makes supersessionism inevitable. Charles resists this conclusion, because Paul never spoke of a thing called "Christianity" that excludes Jews. Paul might see a continuation of Judaism in Christ-faith, but he never refers to the dislodgment of others as a result of it. Charles believes Bird is also guilty of playing on the trope of the heroic, inclusive Paul over and against the villainous, exclusivist Jews. Finally, Charles questions Bird's assertion that Christianity has a "heart" or core theological claim and whether Paul's conception of it must be normative.

Against Witherington, Charles does not think Paul gave an unqual-
ified rejection of his former way of life in Judaism as Witherington
alleges. He also doubts that Paul really believed in the complete abro-
gation of the Torah, as Witherington does. Charles detects a perceived
contradiction in Witherington's view that Paul, on the one hand, no
longer identified as Jewish other than for missional reasons, but on the
other hand considered himself part of the "Israel of God" in Galatians
6:16. He faults a similar (mis)logic in how Witherington understands
Romans 9–11. Finally, Charles wishes Witherington to fill out something he hints at: the possibility of Jews being saved without explicit
faith in Christ.

Final reflections are then offered by Scot McKnight on how he
thinks the conversation has panned out and where he sees the remaining fault lines.

At the risk of generalization, it might be fair to say that some
contributors would heartily endorse Paul's words, "If righteousness
could be gained through the Torah, then the Messiah died for nothing"
(Gal 2:21).[2] In such a statement, Paul arguably asserts that there is a
problem with humanity that finds its solution not in Israel's Torah but
in Israel's Messiah—a solution that not only gentiles need, but even
Israel herself! Other contributors might balk at such a perspective as
wrong, as nothing to do with Jews needing Jesus or replacing Israel, or
as something to be disclaimed to meet the needs of a pluralistic and
multicultural context today. Some contributors might prefer instead
Paul's statement that "God's gifts and his call are irrevocable" (Rom
11:29) as the primary way of summing up Paul's view of Israel. God
loves Israel as his Israel and shall do so until the end of time—to
which one could retort with Galatians 2:21, putting our debate on
a never-ending loop that is, to some degree, of Paul's making. Alas,
Paul himself was trying to affirm God's faithfulness to Israel—and
God sending his Son Jesus to Israel for the sake of the world as the
definitive instance of his faithfulness. That is perhaps the source of

---

2. Scripture quotations in the introduction are the author's translation.

the debate, trying to understand and unpack the meaning of two divine faithfulnesses, to Israel and in Jesus. Such an interpretive task requires a mixture of robust exegesis, sober historical awareness, and interreligious diplomacy. Perhaps a unifying aspect will be found not in the past but in the present, by those who aspire for peace between Greeks, Jews, and the church of God (1 Cor 10:32) and long for a day when God's mercy finds all people (Rom 11:32).

PART 1:
PAULINE
SUPERSESSIONISM
REVISITED

THE SPORT OF SUPERSESSIONISM: A GAME TO BE PLAYED

SCOT MCKNIGHT

There are, it can be said, four versions of the base, bat, and ball game: cricket, played mostly in the United Kingdom and its former colonies; rounders, played mostly in the UK; softball, played mostly in the United States; and baseball, played in the US, Latin America, South America, the Caribbean islands, and eastern Asia. The National Rounders Association claims that rounders has been around since Tudor times and the earliest written evidence is from 1744.[1] Cricket, too, has been argued to derive from Tudor times and, in fact, one can make the case that a reference in 1598 is to a game like the game today called cricket.[2] I shall run right 'round the bases to get to the home conclusion that baseball is a version of rounders, that baseball is mostly an American sport, and that softball is (mostly) an American variation of baseball. One can at least propose—generally accurately, but perhaps to the satisfaction of none—a continuous, progressive history of the base, bat, and ball games from

---

1. "History of the Game," Rounders Online, http://web.archive.org/web/20071112065508/http://www.nra-rounders.co.uk/dyncat.cfm?catid=17177.

2. "Cricket," Wikipedia, http://en.wikipedia.org/wiki/cricket.

cricket to rounders to softball and baseball.[3] One can also compare cricket to rounders to softball and baseball, listing the similarities and dissimilarities, noting the advantages and even superiorities, for a long weekend with friends over beers and have both a good time and create insoluble mysteries.

Back to the base, ball, and bat games. One can argue, as I would do, for the superiority of American baseball. One can, in fact, map the developments and contend that they are improvements to the degree that American baseball surpasses previous historical developments—especially as one considers the speed of the pitching, the sheer brilliance of defensive play, and the almost impossible timing needed to hit a 90-mile-an-hour fastball out of the park for a home run.[4] One can then argue that baseball supersedes the other base, bat, and ball games. One can, as I say, make a case like this, but one will quickly find debate partners, including cricketers and softballers and, though I've not heard this one, a cry from those devoted to rounders. They are "just games" one might say, but those who are devoted to their games don't see them that way. I shall press the case. For the one who is fully devoted to baseball, the other games fall short; for the one devoted to cricket, the others fall short as well.

---

3. Baseball has a wealth of historians and writers and has been called at times the writer's game. I mention only four: Charles C. Alexander, *Our Game: An American Baseball History* (New York: Henry Holt, 1991); G. Edward White, *Creating the National Pastime: Baseball Transforms Itself, 1903–1953* (Princeton: Princeton University Press, 1996); Peter Levine, *A.G. Spalding and the Rise of Baseball: The Promise of American Sport* (New York: Oxford University Press, 1985); Steven A. Riess, ed., *Major Problems in American Sport History: Documents and Essays*, Major Problems in American History (Boston: Houghton Mifflin, 1997). I reveal now that my son played professional baseball in the Cubs organization and is now working in their front office as a scout. Go Cubs!

4. The important study here is by Robert K. Adair, *The Physics of Baseball*, 3rd ed. (New York: Harper Perennial, 2002).

These base, bat, and ball games do not quite rise to the level of religions,[5] but this sketch will serve us well as we seek to unravel the mysteries of supersessionism.

So I move from this game to another one: the seemingly current sport of supersessionism. One might then write a history of Judaism and Christianity and compare the two faiths, just as we have compared these games, but the sport of supersessionism begins the moment one suggests that Jesus and Paul and Christianity *surpass and replace* Judaism. At the level of history unfolding over time, one might play this game—but the moment one's faith and one's destiny and what one thinks God thinks come into play, the game changes, and it all becomes the gravely serious question of truth.

That game is being played today, and I want to contend in this paper that the sport of supersessionism has become a bully club in the hands of some elites. The effect of the club is that now, like being called a capitalist among the Scandinavians or a socialist among America's Republicans, the one thing New Testament scholars don't want to be accused of is "supersessionism." I will ask in this paper that they put the bully club down long enough to admit reality—namely, that the devoted of any of the Abrahamic religions (Judaism, Christianity, Islam) are *inherently particularist*[6] or they diminish their faith with *pluralism*. My claim is not the popular one, so I ask for patience as I seek to unravel the various definitions at work in this new, somewhat aggressive sport. I want, if I may, to throw a slider at the Messianic Jewish believers who are, quite clearly in my judgment, resurrecting the debate Paul had with the Galatians and siding with the Judaizers to form two separate "churches" in the one body of Christ, and I hope the same pitch will have the same results with the religious pluralists

---

5. There are, however, those who think otherwise, and a splendid study here is Christopher H. Evans, *The Faith of 50 Million: Baseball, Religion, and American Culture* (Louisville: Westminster John Knox, 2002).

6. In the case of this paper, then, the term "particularist" means "supersessionist," since we are concerned only with the relation of Judaism and Christianity.

who are, in effect, denouncing as unhistorical what we orthodox really believe happened in history itself. I want to contend that a disinterested approach to the relationship of major world religions can sketch that relationship without recourse to supersessionistic claims, but that the devoted within each Abrahamic religion cannot but be supersessionists (or particularists)—*and that ought to be acceptable for the devoted.* I am, then, using an expansive sense of supersessionism in order to get at one dimension of this argument—namely, the issue of claiming religious truth.[7]

A simple question can be asked from a variety of angles, but it is in effect the same question: Is Christianity's belief in Jesus as God, or the Trinity, a sufficiently restrictive faith (or break) within Judaism to make most or many forms of contemporary Judaism uncomfortable?[8] Is belief in Jesus necessary for salvation for both Jews and gentiles? My contention is that the one who answers with "yes" to each of those questions is inherently supersessionistic. For example, how can one say Jesus is Messiah and not, at some level, be supersessionist in one's faith, in comparison to those who think Jesus is not Messiah?

Before we proceed, I must raise a caution. I am aware that the standard canonical narrative that entails supersessionism has been

---

7. I am grateful to R. Kendall Soulen for suggesting to me that I am expanding the term "supersessionism."

8. The issues here are complex, not only in defining what "Judaism" or a "Jew" is, but also in delineating when or where the so-called "break" occurred. Most scholarship today sees earliest Christianity as a kind of Judaism. That is not our issue. What is has to do with how significant the "difference" is between messianic and nonmessianic Judaisms. On these topics, see Martin Hengel, *Judaism and Hellenism: Studies in Their Encounter in Palestine in the Early Hellenistic Period*, trans. John Bowden, 2 vols. (Philadelphia: Fortress, 1974); James D. G. Dunn, *The Partings of the Ways: Between Christianity and Judaism and Their Significance for the Character of Christianity* (Philadelphia: Trinity Press International, 1991); Shaye J. D. Cohen, *The Beginnings of Jewishness: Boundaries, Varieties, Uncertainties*, Hellenistic Culture and Society 31 (Berkeley: University of California Press, 1999); John J. Collins, *Between Athens and Jerusalem: Jewish Identity in the Hellenstic Diaspora*, rev. ed. (Grand Rapids: Eerdmans, 2000).

used for destructive and diabolical purposes, from the anti-Semitism of the early churches to New World slavery and to the Holocaust and beyond.[9] Any kind of supersessionism that diminishes the integrity of another person, regardless of gender, race, or ethnicity, is the kind of supersessionism that (I would argue) is contrary to the Bible's narratival intent and that therefore deserves to be called *skubala*, rubbish. So one might welcome robust disagreement at the religious level without it entailing diminishment of the personhood of the other. But neither should it turn all truth claims into little more than personal, subjective, cultural and historical preferences.

Scholars of the development of Christianity can speak of a "parting of the ways" and know that dating the moment of that parting is both debatable but over time a fundamental reality. Yes, that parting happened, and it happened over time—and at different times in different places. But if one were to land in medieval Europe, one would know that Christianity and Judaism and Islam are not the same.[10] The parting, I want to hope, can be the opportunity for us to explore the topic of truth.

R. KENDALL SOULEN
AND SUPERSESSIONISM

So far as I know, the most compelling taxonomy of the sorts of supersessionism has been offered by R. Kendall Soulen, professor of systematic theology at Wesley Theological Seminary.[11] At the core of Soulen's proposal is what he calls the "standard canonical narrative,"

---

9. J. Kameron Carter, *Race: A Theological Account* (New York: Oxford University Press, 2008), 11–36.

10. Of the many, I mention only one item here: Dunn, *Partings*.

11. Soulen slightly modified his definitions in the second item listed: R. Kendall Soulen, *The God of Israel and Christian Theology* (Minneapolis: Fortress, 1996); R. Kendall Soulen, "The Standard Canonical Narrative and the Problem of Supersessionism," in *Introduction to Messianic Judaism: Its Ecclesial Context and Biblical Foundations*, ed. David Rudolph and Joel Willitts (Grand Rapids: Zondervan, 2013), 282–91.

and he now thinks the supersessionism at work in that narrative is a "deformation of that narrative, which can be overcome from within, by making it truer to the canon's witness to Jesus Christ and to the Holy Trinity revealed in him."[12] Before we get to this revision, I offer a brief overview of his three sorts of supersessionism from his 1996 book and then an explanation of his 2013 modification.

The standard canonical narrative—creation, fall, redemption in Christ, and consummation (CFRC)—is, Soulen says, inherently supersessionist.[13] How so? "Hence Christ's advent brings about the obsolescence of carnal Israel and inaugurates the age of the spiritual church."[14] In particular, the "written law of Moses is replaced by the spiritual law of Christ, circumcision by baptism, natural descent by faith as criterion of membership in the people of God, and so forth. As a result, *carnal Israel becomes obsolete*."[15] I agree with Soulen that this is one of the standard conclusions of the standard canonical narrative. This leads then to his first kind of supersessionism: the canonical narrative of CFRC is *economic supersessionism*. In this model, Israel is "transient" in its "essential role" in the economic (salvation) history because, once the Messiah comes, the reason for Israel's existence ceases to have a function. To be sure, this term "economic" confuses so many students who suddenly wonder what money has to do with hermeneutics. It refers roughly to periods in God's plan in salvation-history from Israel to the church age. I have never taught a course where "economic" is used like this, either for the Bible's narrative or for the Trinity, where it made intuitive sense to students. So from this point on, I will substitute "salvation-historical" for "economic."

Soulen's second kind of supersessionism is called *punitive supersessionism*.[16] Here the narrative remains more or less the same as is

---

12. Soulen, "Standard Canonical Narrative," 285.

13. Soulen, *God of Israel*, 25–29.

14. Soulen, *God of Israel*, 29.

15. Soulen, *God of Israel*, 29 (italics original).

16. Soulen, *God of Israel*, 30.

found in salvation history, but a grave emphasis comes to the surface—namely, "God abrogates God's covenant with Israel ... on account of Israel's rejection of Christ and the gospel."[17] While punitive supersessionism might seem to be the more serious problem, Soulen thinks the salvation-historical supersessionism "poses a far more difficult problem for Christian theology today."[18] Why? Because it "logically entails the ontological, historical, and moral obsolescence of Israel's existence after Christ."[19] He claims—and on this I think he's right for some framings of the narrative—punitive supersessionism is "little more than an appendix to the standard model's main story line."[20] That is, punitive supersessionism clarifies what is at work in economic supersessionism in the direction of punitive consequences for non-Messianic Judaism. (One might wonder, then, if we even need "punitive" supersessionism in the taxonomy.) The problem, however, is that the salvation-historical narrative that entails punitive supersessionism also entails *structural supersessionism* (the third kind).[21] Here is Soulen's summary: "The standard model is structurally supersessionist *because it unifies the Christian canon in a manner that renders the Hebrew Scriptures largely indecisive for shaping conclusions about how God's purposes engage creation in universal and enduring ways.*"[22]

In essence, then, the problem is the standard canonical narrative, and supersessionism is at work in the grounding and delivery of the narrative itself. Soulen's narrative reveals a fundamental problem in the Christian's standard narrative: it maximizes the universal

---

17. Soulen, *God of Israel*, 30.

18. Soulen, *God of Israel*, 30.

19. Soulen, *God of Israel*, 30.

20. Soulen, *God of Israel*, 30. His point in the use of "appendix" is not that punitive supersessionism is unimportant but that it, in fact, often plays a substantial role in theological arguments.

21. Soulen, *God of Israel*, 31.

22. Soulen, *God of Israel*, 31 (italics original). Terms like "largely indecisive" don't help, for as I read this statement I think of Calvin, who did not think the narrative or its laws were "indecisive" but who almost certainly was supersessionist.

dimensions of the narrative in such a way that it minimizes or deletes the particular dimension of Israel's role in God's plan.[23] That is, by foregrounding the universal, the particular is backgrounded.[24] Here is how Soulen says it: "God's history with Israel does not form an indispensable narrative element of either God's initial work as Consummator or God's work as Redeemer in its definitive form."[25] He says this makes God's work with Israel simply prefigurative, and therefore the background "can be completely omitted from an account of Christian faith without thereby disturbing the overarching logic of salvation history."[26] In practice, Soulen is right: many Christians have no knowledge of the Hebrew Bible and in their practice disparage it. This, it must be said, is how Christianity is practiced by Christians, while many of its thought leaders are hardly as crass.

Soulen's claim is that this standard canonical narrative was formed at the hands of Justin Martyr and Irenaeus, and in his sketch Soulen incontestably adduces evidence for the origins of nothing less than shocking erasures of Israel in the ongoing plan of God.[27] In particular,

---

23. Again, nuance would be appreciated, though Soulen does not attempt to cover all the approaches. Since he does not cover the whole ground, and since I do not want to suggest he is unaware of other narratives, I mention that one influential Reformed narrative is not as harsh as some. Without giving bibliography, the following come to mind: Gerhardus Vos, Abraham Kuyper, Michael Horton, and Michael Bird. Other Christians have a different narrative, one not identical with Soulen's CFRC model, and in some ways escape his accusation but in other ways land on the same problem of the Christian claim that Jesus is the Messiah. See N. T. Wright, *The New Testament and the People of God*, Christian Origins and the Question of God 1 (Minneapolis: Fortress, 1992); N. T. Wright, *Jesus and the Victory of God*, Christian Origins and the Question of God 2 (Minneapolis: Fortress, 1996); N. T. Wright, *Paul and the Faithfulness of God*, 2 vols., Christian Origins and the Question of God 4 (Minneapolis: Fortress, 2013); Scot McKnight, *The King Jesus Gospel: The Original Good News Revisited*, 2nd ed. (Grand Rapids: Zondervan, 2015).

24. Soulen, *God of Israel*, 32.

25. Soulen, *God of Israel*, 32.

26. Soulen, *God of Israel*, 32.

27. It would take us too far afield here, but inherent to Soulen's sketch of a typical Christian reading of the Bible and its story is that it is entirely shaped by soteriology

he finds the quest to demonstrate universalism over against Israel's particularism crucial for the development of this canonical, salvation-historical narrative as explained by Justin Martyr.[28] Furthermore, Justin Martyr saw Israel as transient in the purposes of God. Thus, "For Justin, God's history with the carnal community of the Jews is merely a passing episode within God's more encompassing purposes for creation, which are universal and spiritual in nature."[29] Irenaeus, too, works with a very similar canonical narrative that both maximizes the universal and quarantines the place of Israel in salvation history, even as he gives to Israel an educative mission to the world.[30] At the hands of these two architects of orthodox Christian faith and the standard canonical narrative, the Bible's story is about humans and their salvation. Both thereby consciously know the place of Israel in God's story and yet wipe out the election of Israel after the arrival of Jesus as the Messiah. Soulen frames a crucial dimension of Irenaeus's thinking like this: "Irenaeus subordinates God's identity as the God of Israel to God's identity as Creator and Redeemer of the world in Jesus Christ."[31] The two dimensions of God's salvation history then are the "temporary and prophetic" followed by the "permanent and

---

rather than Christology and ecclesiology. I would contend that a story focusing more on the latter two than simply the first will render a different kind of story, and one that is in some ways less supersessionist. I have sketched that story in McKnight, *King Jesus Gospel*, 136–42, 148–53; Scot McKnight, *Kingdom Conspiracy: Returning to the Radical Mission of the Local Church* (Grand Rapids: Brazos, 2014), 23–35.

28. Soulen, *God of Israel*, 34–40. The push for a universal reading of the Bible's story was also at work in late nineteenth-century and early twentieth-century German scholarship. On the horrors of this scholarship, see (among others) Robert P. Ericksen, *Theologians Under Hitler: Gerhard Kittel, Paul Althaus, and Emanuel Hirsch* (New Haven: Yale University Press, 1985); Susannah Heschel, *The Aryan Jesus: Christian Theologians and the Bible in Nazi Germany* (Princeton: Princeton University Press, 2008); Christopher J. Probst, *Demonizing the Jews: Luther and the Protestant Church in Nazi Germany* (Bloomington: Indiana University Press, 2012).

29. Soulen, *God of Israel*, 37.

30. Soulen, *God of Israel*, 40–48.

31. Soulen, *God of Israel*, 45.

definitive,"[32] themes that clearly are at work in the Lutheran and
Reformed, not to ignore the Anabaptist, reformations. Soulen points
out, and many would agree, that this canonical narrative has within it
an "Israel-forgetfulness."[33] The narrative's fundamental mistake finds
itself in these memorable words by Soulen:[34]

> This perspective obscures the possibility that the Hebrew
> Scriptures are not solely or even primarily concerned with
> the antithesis of sin and redemption but much rather with
> the God of Israel's passionate engagement with the mundane
> affairs of Israel and the nations.

This narrative, however, didn't stop developing late in the second
century but continued to grow and morph. So Soulen takes aim at
Kant and Schleiermacher and then at Barth and Rahner, and only
then turns to a more positive appropriation of the canonical narrative
that focuses on an "economy" of mutual blessing.[35] This systematic
approach to the Bible's narrative, then, is not focused on a separate
but equal relationality but on mutually dependent ways of participating in God's single divine blessing.[36] Hence, Soulen focuses on
difference *and* mutual dependence, not on difference *with* separation.

The Christian asks about Christology, and Soulen delivers his
own approach:

> The gospel is good news about the God of Israel's coming reign,
> which proclaims in Jesus' life, death, and resurrection the victo-
> rious guarantee of God's fidelity to the work of consummation,

---

32. Soulen, *God of Israel*, 46. Soulen thinks "old" and "new" with "testament" are
part of this supersessionist canonical narrative. One ought to note that Paul himself
used such language, though not of the books of the Bible (2 Cor 3:14).

33. Soulen, *God of Israel*, 49–52.

34. Soulen, *God of Israel*, 53.

35. Soulen, *God of Israel*, 109–13.

36. Soulen, *God of Israel*, 134.

that is, to fullness of mutual blessing as the outcome of God's economy with Israel, the nations, and all creation.[37]

But this comes with a correction of colossal proportions, and in my judgment effectively undercuts the Pauline mission (not to mention the Petrine mission): "the church should not confuse its universal mission with a *uniform* mission."[38] That is, the church is commissioned to evangelize the nations (Matt 28:19) but it "has no comparable commission to seek the 'conversion' of the Jewish people."[39] This is a way of saying the church has no need to evangelize Jews—which is a way of saying Paul's missional focus to the Jews first and only then to the gentiles is in need of correction.

In his more recent work, Soulen admits he diminished Christology and the Trinity in his ordering of the canonical narrative and now has contended that the Tetragrammaton—YHWH—is a better place to begin.[40] When Paul says Jesus will be given the name above all names, he is referring to that sacred name—a name that is unfolded trinitarianly into the Giver, Receiver, and Glorifier of the Divine Name. In Soulen's view the non-use of the Divine Name among the earliest Christians testifies not to the obsolescence of Israel's sacred God nor to a supersessionism, but to an affirmation of that God as their God. I'm not so sure this gets one off the hook.

A parallel approach can be found in the theologian Robert Jenson, who describes supersessionism as "the theologoumenon—a doctrine it never was—that the church succeeds Israel in such fashion as to *displace* from the status of God's people those Jews who do not enter

---

37. Soulen, *God of Israel*, 157 (italics original).

38. Soulen, *God of Israel*, 173. One might quibble with the meaning of "uniform" and find cause to disagree in a flexible evangelism, but it does not appear to me that Soulen's concern is there. The next two sentences in my sketch clarify what "uniform" means.

39. Soulen, *God of Israel*, 173.

40. Soulen, "Standard Canonical Narrative," 282–91.

the church"[41] (here he cites approvingly Soulen's work above). Jenson then seems to make a move contrary to Soulen: "The church must indeed call Jews to be baptized into the church of Jews and gentiles and that when this happens it obeys God's will."[42] But then Jenson seems to pull back with this:

> But she [the church] dare not conclude that continuing separate synagogue is *against* God's will. ... Whether the synagogue can in turn recognize the church as belonging to the same people with her is of course another question and one not to be preempted by the church.[43]

The issue of supersessionism is directly connected to the issue of evangelism—and it should be, which provokes consideration of some problems.

PROBLEMS

Soulen points to the core hermeneutical issue at work in the Christian narrative, but I'm not sure he gives enough centrality to the fundamental Christian claim[44]—namely, that the Christian narrative is the hermeneutic development of an existing belief that Jesus of Nazareth is the Messiah, that he was crucified for our sins but raised triumphantly over death as our enemy, and that he is the true ruler of the world. What Christian hermeneutics did was *find a narrative in Israel's Scriptures that led to that fulfillment in Jesus.* Their story was therefore unlike other orderings of Israel's Scriptures because it reordered Israel's narrative in light of Christ, and in so doing saw any other messianic or nonmessianic reordering as *misordered.* Undoubtedly,

---

41. Robert W. Jenson, *The Works of God*, vol. 2 of *Systematic Theology* (New York: Oxford University Press, 1997), 193–94 (italics original).

42. Jenson, *The Works of God*, 193.

43. Jenson, *The Works of God*, 193–94 (italics original).

44. This is a matter of emphasis and centrality; Soulen does claim salvation for the whole world in Christ (e.g., *God of Israel*, 1).

two of the crucial passages at work to create that standard Christian narrative were Romans 5:12–21 and Romans 9–11, not ignoring passages like Matthew 5:17–48 or Galatians 3:15–4:7 or the books of Hebrews and Revelation.

But Soulen's narrative summary lacks the nuances I have come to appreciate in some Christian narratives, so I want to go where he does not go. I agree with Soulen that some, if not too many, operate with a crude supersessionistic narrative, but here I ask a question of what he does not discuss: Why not interact with the finest Christian studies of how the story develops and with those who really do probe the relation of Israel to the church in more beneficial ways? For many in the Christian tradition, it is not the church "replacing" Israel. It becomes far more often a discussion about prophecy and typology and narrative and especially the sense of fulfillment, even *sensus plenior*, and we hear often of the church "expanding" Israel. Yes, the discussion about Israel and church is a massive discussion, but the nuances abound in the history of theology. Again, yes, there is too much supersessionistic language that demeans even the Israel of the Old Testament in some Christian theology, but there have been attempts to hurdle this promise, and these deserve some discussion alongside Soulen's proposals.

For some, "Israel" is not so much made obsolete as swallowed up into what they think the New Testament teaches. In other words, using words like "obsolete" and "replacement" creates a kind of defensive, pejorative rhetoric when terms like "fulfillment" create a more nuanced and accurate rhetoric. Israel of the Old Testament is expanded to be the "Israel of God" (Gal 6:16)—the same old Israel but now different, because gentiles are included in the one people of God (Rom 11:11–24). The law is not so much erased as taken up into, or interpreted by, the revelation of Jesus's Sermon on the Mount (Matt 5:17–20) or Paul's teaching of life in the Spirit (Gal 5:13–26) or in general New Testament "ethics." So, it is not quite as simple as Soulen presents it. Yes, to be sure, some use bold and simple strokes and virtually wipe out Israel, but the best of Christian scholarship is more nuanced and finds a "new" kind of Israel and a "true" Israel as opposed to the balder sense that Israel was for the former days but now we have the (gentile) church.

Yet, I would agree, much of Christian scholarship remains supersessionist but in a far more nuanced manner, and that is why N. T. Wright, in his *Paul and the Faithfulness of God*, comes out swinging against the accusation of supersessionism while affirming a totally Jewish, inner-Judaism kind of *sectarian* supersessionism. One then must ask if there were not all sorts of moments of supersessionism in the canonical narrative: Did Moses supersede Abraham? David supersede Moses? Did Isaiah and Jeremiah and Ezekiel supersede David? At the religious level, we ask if a non-Torah Israelite faith was still Israel's faith after Moses?[45] So, to Wright we now turn.

N. T. WRIGHT AND
SECTARIAN SUPERSESSIONISM

Scholars, or at least New Testament scholars and scholars of earliest Christianity, have dainty egos, so to state what I am about to state will create a stir of disdain among some for raising one scholar above others, but I shall make the statement anyway. N. T. Wright is the most significant New Testament scholar in the world today. His many books are not only read, but he's the target of criticism from all sides, including from postliberals like Douglas Harink who throws an up-and-in fastball at Wright as a supersessionist.[46] In turn, Wright has obviously been stung by some criticisms that he is supersessionist, or that his Paul is painted in too-supersessionist categories, so Wright has not ducked or dived away from the pitch but has come out swinging his bat at that particular pitch.

---

45. One must, of course, recognize the historical-critical discussions here, but the canonical narrative is not the historical-critical story. We concentrate here on the former, as does Soulen.

46. Douglas Harink, *Paul among the Postliberals: Pauline Theology beyond Christendom and Modernity* (Grand Rapids: Brazos, 2003), 151–253.

Wright, in fact, swings hard at this pitch so often that one must step back, read his many statements in context, and then offer summary statements, which is what I shall attempt to do now. The first point to make is that in Wright's grand project, *Paul and the Faithfulness of God*, the whole is suspected as a kind of supersessionism because he thinks Paul has Israel's God "freshly revealed," and the people of God (Israel) "freshly reworked," and Israel's eschatology "freshly imagined."[47] The whole of Paul's mission and theology is a fulfillment theology—that is, Wright thinks Paul sees the scriptures and history coming to their goal in Jesus as Messiah, and everything is reworked in light of Messiah and "spirit" (which, peculiarly, he lowercases). It is precisely here that some scholars find their problem, and it is also precisely here that Wright digs in his feet for his mighty swings. Wright expresses his amazement at the accusation that fulfillment and supersessionism are more or less the same thing in these words:

> We have to contend with what one can only call a revived anti-Christian polemic in which anything, absolutely anything, that is said by way of a 'fulfilment' of Abrahamic promises in and through Jesus of Nazareth is said to constitute, or contribute to, that wicked thing called 'supersessionism', the merest mention of which sends shivers through the narrow and brittle spine of post-modern moralism. How can we say what has to be said, by way of proper historical exegesis, in such a climate?[48]

Notice the point: Wright thinks the accusation that he is a supersessionist (for thinking Paul thought Israel's story had come to its divinely intended goal in the Messiah) is impermissible for a worthy historian's conclusion. He reminds readers of what might be called consensus scholarship's staring eyes before he sketches three kinds of supersessionism:

---

47. These expressions are in the titles for the central three chapters (9–11) of Wright's sketch of Paul's "theology."

48. Wright, *Paul and the Faithfulness of God*, 784.

It has to be said that the charge of 'supersessionism', so readily flung around these days at anyone who has the temerity to
say anything like what Paul was actually saying, needs (to say
the least) to be clarified. Let us suggest three versions at least:
a 'hard' supersessionism, a 'sweeping' supersessionism and a
'Jewish' supersessionism—which last, I shall suggest, does not
deserve the name.[49]

He defines each with ample discussion, but I shall limit myself to
the core statements. First, hard supersessionism is "what we find in
some early Christian writers who, ignoring Paul's warnings in Romans
11 against gentile arrogance, did appear to teach that Jews were now
cast off for ever and that gentile believers had replaced them as the
people of God."[50] Second, sweeping supersessionism is apocalyptic
and even more thorough than hard supersessionism:

> This is the sweeping claim, in line with a certain style of
> post-Barthian (and perhaps 'postliberal') theology, that what
> happened in Jesus Christ constituted such a radical inbreaking
> or 'invasion' into the world that it rendered redundant anything
> and everything that had gone before—particularly anything
> that looked like 'religion', not least 'covenantal religion'. This
> view is unlike 'hard supersessionism' because it denies that
> there is any historical continuity at all: it isn't that 'Israel' has
> 'turned into the church', but rather that Israel, and everything
> else prior to the apocalyptic announcement of the gospel, has
> been swept aside by the fresh revelation.[51]

---

49. Wright, *Paul and the Faithfulness of God*, 806.

50. Wright, *Paul and the Faithfulness of God*, 806–7.

51. Wright, *Paul and the Faithfulness of God*, 807. Everything in this paragraph
by Wright is aimed at apocalyptic Paul scholarship.

Wright points his bat at Ernst Käsemann and J. L. Martyn, and I find his critique of this apocalyptic approach to Paul on target when it comes to its own version of supersessionism. So Wright contends that Paul, like the Qumran writings, has a *sectarian* supersessionism. In fact, in a note Wright quotes the Jewish scholar Jon D. Levenson, who said, "Nowhere does Christianity betray its indebtedness to Judaism *more than in its supersessionism*"![52] In passing, this is the kind of nuance in story and narrative and history that is completely missed by Soulen. Wright explains this Jewish supersessionism in this way:

> In other words, Judaism has always contained a narrative pattern in which a late-born son supplants older brothers, or a new movement (such as Qumran) claims to represent or embody the true people of God. One could even regard the Mishnah as 'supersessionist', since it sketches a way of being Jewish which many Jews of earlier generations would neither have recognised nor approved.[53]

Here is how Wright defines sectarian supersessionism:

> This is the claim that the creator God has acted at last, in surprising but prophecy-fulfilling ways, to launch his renewed covenant, to call a new people who are emphatically in continuity with Abraham, Isaac and Jacob, to pour out his spirit afresh upon them, to enable them to keep Torah in the new way he had always envisaged and to assure them that he and his angels were present with them in their worship (even though they were not in the Jerusalem temple) and that their united community was to be seen as the real focal point of 'Israel'. Members of the Qumran community were of course all Jews, but most Jews were not members of the community.

---

52. Wright, *Paul and the Faithfulness of God*, 809n110 (italics added).
53. Wright, *Paul and the Faithfulness of God*, 809n110.

Other Jews were at liberty to join, by means of (as with most
monastic communities) a process of testing and probation-
ary periods. They would have to take upon themselves the
special responsibilities of this new community, and live up to
them. Members of this community saw the rest of the Jewish
world as dangerously compromised, with even the zealous
Pharisees being 'speakers of smooth things', and (depending
on your theory) some at least of the priestly class totally compromised and corrupt.[54]

Wright, however, not only swings at this pitch but decides to do
what many would say is impossible: he turns from swinging the bat
to pitching the ball. That is, he argues that *not only is Paul a sectarian
supersessionist, but it is silly to call this supersessionism!* His words now:

Is this position 'supersessionism' in any meaningful sense? A
case could be made for using that word. But, unlike the two
previous models, in both of which there is a definite sense of
replacement of Israel and everything it stood for with something quite new, there is here a characteristically Jewish note
of fulfilment. It would be extremely odd if, in a group whose
whole existence depended on being the people of a prom-
ise-making God, nobody was ever allowed to claim that the
promises had been fulfilled, for fear of being called 'supersessionist'. Was John the Baptist a 'supersessionist'? Was Jesus?
The claim could of course be challenged: your idea of 'fulfilment' doesn't fit with ours, or the events that you claim constitute 'fulfilment' don't look like what we expected to see under
that heading, and therefore your claim is falsified. But the idea
that such a claim could never be made looks as if it is cutting
off the branch on which its entire worldview had been sitting.
I submit that the oddity of calling Qumran theology 'supersessionist', granted the sense which that somewhat sneering term

---

54. Wright, *Paul and the Faithfulness of God*, 809.

has come to bear, is so great that we should probably think of a different way of describing such a worldview.[55]

Maybe, he suggests on the same page, we should "call it 'Jewish supersessionism' if you like, but recognize the oxymoronic nature of such a phrase." He then comes up and in on his opponents:

> The scandal of Paul's gospel, after all, was that the events in which he claimed that Israel's God had been true to what he promised centred on a crucified Messiah. That is the real problem with any and all use of the 'supersession' language: either Jesus was and is Israel's Messiah, or he was not and is not. That question in turn is of course directly linked to the question of the resurrection: either Jesus rose from the dead or he did not. Trying to use postmodern moralism, with its usual weapon of linguistic smearing, as a way to force Christians today to stop saying that Jesus was Israel's Messiah is bad enough, though that is not our current problem. Trying to use that moralism as a way of forcing first-century historians to deny that Paul thought Jesus was the Messiah, and that the divine promises to Israel had been fulfilled in him, simply will not do.[56]

Put differently, a messianic Jew like Paul—one who thinks Jesus is the Messiah and was crucified yet raised by God from among the dead—must think in terms of fulfillment of Israel's story and must think in terms of revision, reworking, and refreshing that same old story made new, and must now think in terms of the fate of those who don't embrace that Messiah. Wright again:

> If Paul really did believe that Jesus was Israel's Messiah— and the paragraph, not to mention the rest of Paul's writing, makes no sense unless we see that belief at its heart—then it is impossible to imagine him, or any second-temple Jew in a

---

55. Wright, *Paul and the Faithfulness of God*, 809–10.
56. Wright, *Paul and the Faithfulness of God*, 810.

comparable position, supposing that this Messiah could have
his followers while 'Israel' could carry on as though nothing
had happened. That, indeed, would be the route to the true
'supersessionism': the idea that Jesus had started a new movement discontinuous with Israel's history from Abraham to the
present. To claim, instead, that this history is affirmed, vali-
dated and now fulfilled, however surprisingly, by the arrival
of Israel's Messiah—to call this 'supersessionism' is a cynical
misuse of words. Was Akiba 'supersessionist' when he hailed
bar-Kochba as Messiah and summoned Israel to rally to the
flag? Paul is indicating a messianic identity and way of life
which he sees as genuine worship of the God of Israel—only
without circumcision and other Torah-badges. That is the paradox which characterizes Paul at every point.[57]

This for Wright is a matter of history and a task for historians. He
can say it no more strongly than this:

This means that we must recognize some recent slogans for
what they are. When people talk, as they often do these days, of
'replacement' theologies in which something called 'the church'
replaces something called 'the Jews', or 'Israel'; when people talk,
as they sometimes do, of 'substitution' theologies, in which 'the
church' (again!) has substituted for 'Israel' or 'the Jews' in the
divine plan; when they refer to a position in which 'the church'
has displaced 'Israel'; when they talk, above all, of that unfortu-
nate word 'supersession', in which 'the church'—and often the
gentile church at that—has superseded 'the Jews' or 'Israel'—there
we are witnessing something which, while it may have been true
of much later generations, was not and could not have been
true for Paul. For Paul it was dazzlingly clear. Either Jesus was
Israel's Messiah or he was not. Tertium non datur.[58]

57. Wright, Paul and the Faithfulness of God, 985–86.
58. Wright, Paul and the Faithfulness of God, 1412.

One of the more vocal critics of Wright's approach comes from a group of scholars who sometimes refer to themselves as "post-new perspective" and most importantly as "post-supersessionist," the second claim taking of course the high moral ground. Wright swings at their pitches too, in these words:

> Some, like Ed Sanders, have seen it as obvious that Paul viewed 'the church' as a 'third entity'. ... The suggestion of a 'third race' has provoked strong reactions. The editors of a recent collection of essays on 'Paul and Judaism', discovering that one of their contributors actually believes more or less what Sanders had argued thirty years ago, describe this in the shocked tones of an elegant lady discovering that her favourite nephew is going to marry a chorus girl. 'Bird,' they say, 'actually thinks that the new group of Jesus believers could be conceived of as a third race'. In the same vein, [David] Rudolph declares that what he calls 'the consensus reading', according to which Paul belonged to 'the "third entity" church', reinforces the view that Pauline Christianity 'was an anti-Jewish movement', leading 'to the delegitimisation of Jewish existence and to the erasure, or displacement, of Jews from the church'. *This kind of rhetorical overplaying of the hand does historical exegesis no good.* Rudolph, [Mark] Nanos and many others are reacting obviously and naturally to the bitter experience of Jewish people in Europe and elsewhere for many generations, but one cannot decide first-century meanings that way, any more than one can force Paul to adjudicate a debate between Luther and Calvin. This so-called 'post-supersessionist' position, however, is itself well on the way to becoming a new 'consensus'. The protests that have been raised against it (pointing out that when Paul faced potential anti-Judaism in Rome he did it by arguing that Jewish people could and would return, in faith, to 'their own olive tree', in other words, that the real 'anti-Judaism' would be to deny Jews a place in the messianic company of Abraham's worldwide

family) have fallen on deaf ears. This is not what people want
to hear. But, as with questions of Pauline doctrinal teaching,
it will not do to highlight features of a much later, and totally
different, world and use them as Procrustean beds to force
Paul into shape. That merely reproduces the worst features
of a former ecclesiastical control to which historical exegesis
rightly objected. History matters.[59]

The last comment in Wright's big work finishes with a flourish that
sets the whole discussion in context: "For Paul, there was only one
olive tree, because there was only one God; and the divine purposes,
though wise beyond human imaginings, were fully revealed in Israel's
Messiah, the crucified and risen Jesus of Nazareth. The 'identity' of
the Messiah's people was thus grounded, like everything else in Paul's
thought, in the faithfulness of Israel's God."[60]

Anyone who cares not only about the concrete social and ecclesial realities of the first-century churches but also about church life
today can be excused if, after reading books like either Soulen's or
Wright's, that same person might still be wondering what it was *really*
like and what it is *supposed* to be like today. Some strategies appear
to be a mutual toleration of complementary religions (play any of the
bat, ball, and base games), and Wright's appears to be much more
of a fusion of cultures in a new ecclesial reality. That is, it appears to
me that Wright thinks the Pauline churches had thoroughly mixed
assemblies, or house churches, and that former identities, including
the ethnic and racial identity of being Jewish, surrendered themselves
to fellowship in the church. That is, Jewish believers no more ceased
being Jewish than males ceased being male, but *those identity markers* were swallowed up into the *new identity in Christ in a new creation.*
I'm not the first to wonder aloud, after hearing sketches like those of

---

59. Wright, *Paul and the Faithfulness of God*, 1444, 1445.

60. Wright, *Paul and the Faithfulness of God* 1449.

Wright, whether Paul and Jewish believers in Jesus as Messiah were Torah-observant—or at least to ask how Torah-observant they were. This issue matters deeply in current supersessionism conversations, so I need yet again to quote extensively from Wright, because his way of conceptualizing Paul's Jewishness strikes the post-new-perspective and post-supersessionism caucus as yet another instance of supersessionism (at least for one way of being Jewish). After establishing that Paul thought of himself as Jewish (Rom 9:1–5; 11:1; Gal 2:15–21), here is Wright's principal way of framing Paul's Jewish identity:

> Would Paul's Jewish contemporaries have considered him a 'Jew'? This is not just about things that he believed. Many Jews no doubt believed many strange things, including the identification of strange people as 'Messiahs'. But Jews then as now have seldom made niceties of 'belief' the main criterion. The question would have been, what was he doing, or perhaps not doing? Paul admitted people to Abraham's family without requiring the covenant sign of circumcision. Paul spoke of the 'temple', referring not now to the shrine in Jerusalem but to the fellowship of Jesus-followers and even to individuals among them. Paul treated the Messiah-faith 'family' as an extended family, insisting on people 'marrying within' that family in the way he would previously have insisted on Jewish endogamy. Paul does not seem to have bothered about the sabbath, regarding it as something that Messiah-followers could observe or not as they chose. All this must have raised not only eyebrows but also hackles among the Jewish populations in the Diaspora.

Notoriously, Paul went further. He shared table fellowship with non-Jews who were Messiah-believers. If that caused problems even for Peter and Barnabas, as it seems to have done (we can hardly suppose that Paul invented the awkward "Antioch incident" out of thin air), we can be sure that it would have caused serious problems for the young Saul of Tarsus. He advised the Messiah-people in Corinth to accept dinner invitations from anyone and everyone, and

to eat unquestioningly what was provided, the only exception being
if someone's conscience was still "weak" at the thought of eating idol-
meat. Not only, then, did he advocate eating with uncircumcised and
even with unbelieving gentiles, but on an apparently straightforward
reading of the relevant passages (we shall discuss them further in a
moment) he advocated, in principle, eating their nonkosher food, on
the scriptural grounds that "the earth and its fullness belong to the
lord."[61]

These two paragraphs, I am arguing, will be seen by some today as
the tipping point revealing that Wright has fallen again into supersessionism, and Wright would no doubt come back and say, "No, this is
Judaism, perhaps sectarian supersessionism, but still Judaism reshaped
around one driving conviction—that Jesus was raised from the dead
and is the Messiah. Paul is but one example of a very Jewish thing to
do." Wright digs in with what I suspect will be memorable words:[62]

> I can understand people who are rightly concerned for
> Christian–Jewish relations today struggling with this text. I
> can understand people trying to imagine that it was maybe a
> rhetorical overstatement. What I cannot understand is people
> trying to make an argument that Paul was in some sense a
> Torah-observant Jew but not even mentioning this major piece
> of counter-evidence. Nor can I understand someone suggest-
> ing that for Paul to recognize Jesus as Messiah 'did not mean
> any repudiation of the Torah.' If 'dying to something' is not
> repudiating it, Paul's words have no meaning.

Wright expands this discussion, but this is all we need for the
moment. The point I want to make is not whether I agree with Wright
but whether this is supersessionism (which Wright says it is—sectarian but not hard supersessionism) and what this looked like on
the ground. As I see it, Wright thinks Jewish believers flexed in their

---

61. Wright, *Paul and the Faithfulness of God*, 1428–29.

62. Wright, *Paul and the Faithfulness of God*, 1430.

Torah observation because their identity had shifted—or better yet, their Jewish identity had been fulfilled "in Christ." Paul determined his Torah-observance by context, and he would have expected other Jewish believers to discern in the same manner.

But not all in this sport of supersessionism agree. Some think Tom has rendered cricket and rounders obsolete.

MARK KINZER AND
BILATERAL ECCLESIOLOGY

Mark Kinzer offers Soulen's essential stance against supersessionism of all kinds, but as a Messianic Jew and historian of earliest Christianity, he proposes a different solution than what one finds in Wright.[63] So, if supersessionism fails the plan of God, what becomes of the people of God, Israel, when Jesus is seen as Messiah? What becomes of Jewish identity and Torah-observance for the Jewish believer in Jesus? For Kinzer, those early decades of the Jesus movement entailed a bilateral ecclesiology. That is, Jesus is indeed the Messiah and Lord for Jews and gentiles, but Israel's God remains faithful to the promises to Israel so that Israel is not replaced; it has a distinctive calling, and that calling for the nation of Israel obtains after Jesus and in spite of rejecting Jesus as Messiah.

More particularly—and for many of us, this is the alarming part—for Kinzer the church has two branches (but not two covenants): a Jewish church and a gentile church, a unity in the church that simultaneously retains Israel's distinctive callings and a unity that also entails separation into separate kinds of churches. (Church history, from the second century to the Holocaust, destroyed such an arrangement and, in particular, the attraction of Jews to Jesus and the church.) Israel—that is, Jews as a whole—are still the object of God's love and calling; God has sent the Messiah in Jesus, but for the sake of gentiles there is

63. Mark S. Kinzer, *Post-Missionary Messianic Judaism: Redefining Christian Engagement with the Jewish People* (Grand Rapids: Brazos, 2005); a brief summary is found at 151–53.

a hardening in part in order to give opportunity for gentiles to enter into the "church." The Jewish believers (the remnant) remain fully Jewish, connected to the Jewish community but also fully Torah-observant, and so are a leavening presence to Israel that, in its priestly role, sanctifies all of Israel, while the gentile believers are to form their connection to God's promise to Israel through their fellowship with the Jewish church.

Even more, Kinzer proposes—rather astonishingly, I suspect, to nonmessianic Jews—that Jesus remains present among the Jewish people whether they know it or not.[64] His words:

> We must be able to affirm that Yeshua abides in the midst of the Jewish people and its religious tradition, despite that tradition's apparent refusal to accept his claims.[65]

But I see absolutely no ground for separating Jews and gentiles like this in Pauline house churches, and it is not a little ironic that this bilateral ecclesiology leads many of us to wonder if the situation Paul opposed so vehemently in Galatians is not lurking in this approach.[66] Nonetheless, this post-supersessionistic approach has gained traction today, not least because it appeals to contemporary instincts for pluralism.

But let me add this: Yes, by all means I want to raise up the importance of Messianic Judaism and its potential witness in the Jewish

---

64. Kinzer, *Post-Missionary Messianic Juadism*, 213–33. Below I will argue for "salvific" supersessionism. At this point, I'd say Kinzer's posing of a Jesus present in the Jewish community is a way of affirming nothing less than salvific supersessionism. That is, he thinks salvation is in Jesus alone.

65. Kinzer, *Post-Missionary Messianic Judaism*, 217. A similar kind of colonialism occurs in Irving Greenberg, who colonizes Christianity as Judaism for the gentiles. See Irving Greenberg, *For the Sake of Heaven and Earth: The New Encounter Between Judaism and Christianity* (Philadelphia: Jewish Publication Society, 2004), 213–34.

66. For a sympathetic but solid critique of Kinzer on the basis of Thomist thinking, see Holly Taylor Coolman, "Christological Torah," *Studies in Christian-Jewish Relations* 5 (2010): 1–12.

community, and I also want to add that they alone probably can effect this kind of witness. Furthermore, *on the merits of their own witness* they remind gentile Christians of the vitality of God's promises to Israel as a people and of God's continued faithfulness to that people. If I find separate churches unfaithful to the Pauline mission of churches marked by unity of all sorts (Gal 3:28), I do not do so by way of diminishing the reality of the Jewish identity of messianic Jews. I celebrate that identity.

SALVIFIC SUPERSESSIONISM

I want to move this discussion, however, out of the realm of analogies and history and into theology. There are places of agreement and disagreement with those I have sketched above. I join hands with Soulen who is doing—if I read him aright—constructive and normative theology, even if I differ with him substantively on what is normative. I follow most of what Wright says, especially the need to probe the significance of "sectarian" supersessionism, even if I differ with Wright in particular on how he understands Torah-observance among Jewish believers in the first century. I also think Kinzer may have put his finger on how the first Jesus movement worked at times, but I think his framework is too rigidly committed to Torah-observance and cannot adequately explain either 1 Corinthians 9:19–23 or how Galatians works. Put differently, Soulen sees two divided communities that are designed by God to be a unity, Wright sees a "third race" in the church, while Kinzer finds two kinds of church. I am closest, then, to Wright. I see the church as Israel expanded (and fulfilled, and therefore a new people with deep dimensions of continuity) in which Jewish believers will remain sometimes Torah-observant and gentile believers not Torah-observant except in general, but that they will form one fellowship—and I mean one local church that worships, teaches, and eats together—and will share the table together (kosher folks eating with nonkosher folks, and sometimes kosher folks not eating kosher). Thus, I agree with Wright that Jews and gentiles *will sit in mixed table fellowship* and so transcend difference in a new-creation kind of unity through the power of the Spirit. I agree, too, with Wright in that "fulfillment in Christ" marks the new identity more than anything else. That there is neither Jew nor Greek in Christ means those ethnic identities will lead not to separation but to ethnicity-transcending *koinonia* at the table.

The issue, I contend, is deeper than the disinterestedness these discussions sometimes mask; the issue driving these discussions is *truth—ultimate religious truth*—and it is often latent or buried under the historical discussions.

I contend, then, that this discussion can be discussed in another way, and it is about truth. Is Jesus the Messiah? If he is, then the game of truth must be played. If Jesus is the Messiah, and if Jesus is the Messiah of both Jews (what other kind of "Messiah" could there be?) and of gentiles (the singular Pauline mystery), and if Jesus was raised from the dead and now rules as King and Lord, and if this Jewish and gentile Messiah-King is the one who by virtue of his life, death, resurrection, and exaltation brings redemption to all who are "in Christ," then we have a more refined sense of supersessionism, which I call *salvific* supersessionism. I contend, in a similar way to the Jewish scholar David Novak, that Christianity is inherently supersessionistic in this sense (Novak calls this "soft" supersessionism).[67] How so? Salvific supersessionism makes the bold truth claim that the New Testament affirms that salvation is found only in Christ.

What Wright calls "sectarian" supersessionism, then, needs a slight adjustment to salvific supersessionism, so that this kind of supersessionism is inherently Jewish. That is, as Moses superseded Abraham, and David Moses, and Isaiah all the prophets before him; as the Pharisees superseded the Sadducees, and the Essenes the Pharisees, and the rabbis the Pharisees, so Jesus and Paul and Peter and John were *Jewish and therefore supersessionistic hermeneuts*. Levenson puts

---

67. David Novak, "The Covenant in Rabbinic Thought," in *Two Faiths, One Covenant? Jewish and Christian Identity in the Presence of the Other*, ed. Eugene B. Korn (Lanham, MD: Rowman and Littlefield, 2004), 65–80.

it even more dramatically, so I repeat: "For the longstanding claim of the Church that it supersedes the Jews, in large measure continues the old narrative pattern in which a late-born son dislodges his first-born brothers, with varying degrees of success. Nowhere does Christianity betray its indebtedness to Judaism more than in its supersessionism."[68] The game of truth cannot eschew the summons to "gospel" all—Jews and gentiles—to Jesus. Both Jews and gentiles are summoned to find redemption alone "in Christ."

The game of truth not only asks whether Jesus is the Messiah, but it asks about the relation of Israel to the church, and I contend Paul's image in Romans 11:11–24 is the image we most need in order to know Paul's message. Before a few brief observations, we should know that this text haunts the second century's volatile and disastrous distancing of the church from its Jewish (and Old Testament) roots and the turning of the Christian faith and all of orthodoxy away from the essential Israelite story, creating a situation in which, to be fair to Paul on this issue of the church and Israel, we must be able to get behind the second century.[69] But there is another side to Romans 11:11–24: Paul's words entail a grievous message as well. First, Paul thinks Israel (he's talking here about contemporary Jews who encountered Jesus and know the message he proclaims) has failed to receive their God-sent Messiah. Paul calls this failure "stumbling" (11:11–12). Their stumbling, however, has resulted in gentile inclusion. Second, Paul holds out hope (11:23), which proves he's not a hard, sweeping, economic, punitive, or structural supersessionist. There is clearly a place in Paul's thought for (ethnic) Israel—the Israel that received God's inviolable covenant promise and for whom that promise remains, but Paul knows they must believe in Jesus in order to

---

68. Jon D. Levenson, *The Death and Resurrection of the Beloved Son: The Transformation of Child Sacrifice in Judaism and Christianity* (New Haven: Yale University Press, 1995), x.

69. This is not the place to discuss this disastrous distancing; see Kinzer, *Post-Missionary Messianic Judaism*, 181–212.

inherit that promise. Third, if there is a punitive dimension to Paul's kind of salvific supersessionism, it is the punishment incurred by rejecting Jesus as Messiah. That is, some of the branches in the tree trunk called Israel have been broken off (11:17). I don't know how to avoid some implications of the punitive in this kind of language from Paul. Fourth, gentile believers are grafted into the tree trunk called Israel. Israel is not done away with; Israel is not superseded; Israel is *expanded to include gentiles*. This cannot be called supersessionism in the traditional sense that concerns Soulen. Yet, fifth, the critical factor for Paul here is the Messiah, who revolutionizes because he fulfills Israel's story, and he revolutionizes because everything is reconfigured around him; one must believe in him to be part of what Paul means by Israel (now expanded) (11:20). This is the crucial element of *salvific* supersessionism. Sixth, so important to Paul in Romans— and, I think, in many ways driving the whole of his letter—is the strong claim that gentile believers *have no right to diminish Israel (or Jews)* (11:17–20). This is the very thing most forms of supersessionism, as illustrated above in Soulen and Wright, have done in church history, and it is the very reason Paul writes this great letter: to show that God is still faithful to Israel when Israel's God includes gentiles in the people of God.[70]

If the gentile believers are warned by Paul not to diminish the covenant God has made with Israel, so the Jewish believers are warned not to segregate or separate themselves from gentile believers. This is the undeniable teaching of Peter's famous incident involving table fellowship with gentiles in Galatians 2:11–14. Fellowship with difference is the implication of Acts 15. For the apostle Paul, the ecclesia is a mixture of Jews and gentiles, slave and free, men and women, who now have an ecclesial unity and an ecclesial identity in Christ (Gal 3:28). Most importantly, this ecclesia of Paul is not a gentile group but a mixing of Jews and gentiles who believe in the Messiah at one table

---

70. Scot McKnight, *Reading Romans Backwards: A Gospel of Peace in the Midst of Empire* (Waco, TX: Baylor University Press, 2019).

and around one table. Hence, the recent protests of the post-super-sessionist messianic Jewish thinkers who contend there needs to be bilateral ecclesiology—one ecclesia for Jewish believers and another ecclesia for gentile believers—both resurrects the so-called Judaizing wing of the letter of Paul to the Galatians and creates a massive fissure in the one people of God, the church that is Israel expanded. Too much of post-supersessionistic theology then is theological fracking. Here is how Mark Kinzer defines this bilateral ecclesia: this new reality "can only be lived viably in an *ekklēsia* that consists of two distinct but united corporate bodies—a Jewish and a gentile *ekklēsia*. The Jewish *ekklēsia* would live as a part of the wider Jewish community, and the gentile *ekklēsia* would express its solidarity with the Jewish people through its loving bond with the Jewish *ekklēsia*."[71] While no one would contest that first-century churches in the Holy Land were entirely (or almost entirely) Jewish and most likely Torah-observant, and that over time the bulk of Roman Empire churches were mostly gentile, at issue in Kinzer's bilateral ecclesia is when Jews and gentiles in the same community are forming separate, segregated churches. I find this a denial of the very mission of the apostle Paul. For him, Jesus is the Messiah of both Jews and gentiles, and they are to form one fellowship, the church, because of Jesus's universal lordship. There is in Christ—the central claim of Paul—a new reality formed, a new people of God that expands Israel-prior-to-the-Messiah.

It is not possible here to explore and exegete the various New Testament texts that deserve to be brought into play, so I hold myself to a few brief observations. Colossians 1:15–20 is supersessionist in several directions at once: Christ supersedes Adam (as *eikon*), Christ supersedes the figure of Wisdom in Proverbs 8, Christ supersedes Jewish wisdom traditions, Christ supersedes middle Platonism's creation traditions, Christ supersedes Roman and Greek and Jewish political authorities and powers, and he supersedes as creator and the firstborn among the dead. Jesus's death redeems and his resurrection establishes a new-creation

---

71. Kinzer, *Post-Missionary Messianic Judaism*, 23, 151–79.

order in and through him for the sake of Israel and the world. But for
the Paul of Colossians, the ecclesia is a profoundly new mixing of Jews
and gentiles, something Paul calls the mystery—a mystery established
on the basis of Christology, a Christology expressed in a soteriology,
what I am calling a salvific supersessionism.

This christological claim is as simple as it is old: "I am the way,
the truth and life. No one comes to the Father except through me"
(John 14:6).[72] Now it might take pages to unpack the exegesis, but
the driving point is not hard to admit: John's Gospel contends access
to God the Father is through Jesus and through Jesus alone. Peter, in
the book of Acts, makes a very similar claim: "There is salvation in no
one else, for there is no other name under heaven among mortals by
which we must be saved" (Acts 4:12). Now Paul's haunting words for
this whole salvific supersessionist discussion, from Romans 10:1–4:

> Brothers and sisters, my heart's desire and prayer to God for
> them [the Israelites, so NIV] is that they may be saved. I can
> testify that they have a zeal for God, but it is not enlightened.
> For, being ignorant of the righteousness that comes from God,
> and seeking to establish their own, they have not submitted to
> God's righteousness. For Christ is the end of the law so that
> there may be righteousness for everyone who believes.

I believe the issue driving some of the supersessionistic accusations and the post-supersessionistic readings is pluralism—religious pluralism—and the accusation and readings are either denials
or attempts to explain away a claim the New Testament makes from
the beginnings of its record: that Jesus is the Messiah and that in him
alone salvation is found and that in him we are to find one new Body
of both Jews and gentiles. The question to ask the one who uses the
term "supersessionism" is: Do you think Jesus is the Messiah and do
you think salvation is found in him alone? The answer to that question will determine how one will use the term "supersessionism."

---

72. Scripture quotations in this essay are the author's translation.

PAUL'S MESSIANIC ESCHATOLOGY AND SUPERSESSIONISM

MICHAEL F. BIRD

Several years ago, I was teaching a church history class in which I read to students excerpts from John Chrysostom's eight homilies against the Jews. As I read aloud to the students, inflecting my voice, and modulating my tone for dramatic effect, I would occasionally look up and notice that their faces were contorting with expressions of confusion and disgust. Immediately after, they asked me questions like, "How could a Christian say things like that?" and "Why does Chrysostom hate the Jews so much?" And therein we began a long and painful discussion about the history of Jewish and Christian relations that eventually came to the apostle Paul.

The grist for the mill is Paul's conception of his gentile, Christ-believing assemblies vis-à-vis "Israel," with Israel understood as both (1) the historical people in relationship to God as narrated in the Hebrew Bible and (2) the empirical expression of Israel as contemporary Jews of Judea and the diaspora. My thesis is that Paul does indeed think of his gentile assemblies as belonging to "Israel," as they are grafted into God's covenant people when they are grafted into Israel's Messiah. To be "in Messiah" is to be "in Israel"! The notion that gentiles could join the Jewish commonwealth as proselytes was widely accepted and periodically pursued.[1] However, where Paul is different—we might even say anomalous—is his insistence that God has acted in the Messiah to effect the inclusion of gentiles into Israel without the normal rituals for conversion (circumcision) nor requiring complete adherence to the Torah as the mark of allegiance to God (law-observance). For Paul, the end of the ages has come in the Messiah's death and resurrection and will yet erupt further when the Messiah returns. It is amidst this transition of the ages that the boundaries of and basis for belonging to Israel have been altered. What determines one's position before God and in God's people is faith in the Messiah, life in the Spirit, and keeping God's commandments for both gentiles and Jews.[2]

Paul's "messianic eschatology" seems to necessitate some variety of supersessionism, with Paul believing that Israel is redefined around the Messiah and the Spirit. This is an inescapable inference given that Paul believed he was right and his fellow Jews were wrong. They were wrong about Jesus as the crucified and exalted Lord, wrong about whether the end was here and nigh, wrong about how gentiles could be reconciled to God, wrong to oppose his message and ministry among Jews and gentiles, and wrong about the lines that separated the faithful from the apostate in this new age.[3] Paul is supersessionist in the sense that he is sectarian; he believes that his view of God,

---

1. See Scot McKnight, *A Light Among the Gentiles: Jewish Missionary Activity in the Second Temple Period* (Minneapolis: Fortress, 1991); Michael F. Bird, *Crossing Over Sea and Land: Jewish Missionary Activity in the Second Temple Period* (Peabody, MA: Hendrickson, 2010).

2. I argue at length for this in Michael F. Bird, *An Anomalous Jew: Paul among Jews, Greeks, and Romans* (Grand Rapids: Eerdmans, 2016). Several issues also are addressed in Michael F. Bird, "N. T. Wright and Paul's Supersessionism: A Response to Kaminsky and Reasoner," *Harvard Theological Review* 113.4 (2020): 498–512.

3. Even Douglas A. Campbell's so-called *beyond supersessionism* view still stipulates that Paul's fellow Jews had made "some very serious mistakes—rejecting Jesus, the incarnation of their God, being one of them, something he holds them fully responsible for" and that their "sacred-nation theology" has fallen under "judgment" and needed to be "radically reformed or eliminated." See Douglas A. Campbell,

gentiles, Messiah, the end, covenant fidelity, and community boundaries should be the norm in Jewish communities.

However, the mere mention of supersessionism causes umbrage
and alarm. Have we now given succour to Chrysostom and his Jew-
hating tirades that God has renounced the Jews and replaced them
with Christians? Personally, I hope not! But we cannot avoid the
inevitability of supersessionism in Paul, and we do best to offer a
refined analysis of it and then make an informed response to it. In
this essay, I intend to exposit the contours of Paul's supersessionism
in light of modern scholarship, to state what it is and is not, with a
view to hopefully understanding how Paul relates to non-Christ-believing Jews. Beyond that, those of us who live in the Christian tradition may thereafter use the resources of our Scriptures to face the
history of Christian anti-Semitism and to develop a praxis for living
in a religiously pluralistic world.

SUPERSESSIONISM IN SCHOLARSHIP

An immediate observation is that "supersession" is often deployed in
scholarly discussion premised on the notion that its mere mention
constitutes a form of refutation. Supersessionism becomes a type
of red card or flag thrown down to indicate a foul.[4] In effect, "the
merest mention" of "supersessionism," says N. T. Wright, "sends shiv-
ers through the narrow and brittle spine of post-modern moralism."[5]
Scot McKnight prosecutes the same point with even more rigor: "it
has become sport to call the other options in Pauline scholarship a
grand example of supersessionism," and "it is enough for some to gain
the upper hand, like progressives and conservatives in some political

---

Pauline Dogmatics: The Triumph of God's Love (Grand Rapids: Eerdmans, 2020), 708
(688–719).

4. See Douglas Harink, "Paul and Israel: An Apocalyptic Reading," *Pro Eclessia*
16 (2007): 359–80.

5. N. T. Wright, *Paul and the Faithfulness of God*, Christian Origins and the
Question of God 4 (London: SPCK, 2014), 784; see also N. T. Wright, *Pauline
Perspectives: Essays on Paul, 1978–2013* (Minneapolis: Fortress, 2013), 403.

battle, by all but damning the other with the S-word."[6] I submit that aversion to supersessionism tells us more about the sociology of religious scholarship than it does about the designation itself.

The immediate problem with treating supersessionism as an intellectual opprobrium is that supersessionism is multifarious, not monolithic. Which supersessionism are we talking about and censuring? One might (rightfully!) denounce supersessonism as "the belief that the church has taken the place of the Jews as the elect people of God."[7] But there are several species of supersessionism available. Some prefer to differentiate hard versus soft varieties of supersessionism.[8] Others prefer a taxonomy of economic, punitive, and structural supersessionisms.[9] Wright refers to "hard," "sweeping," and "Jewish" versions of supersessionism.[10] But if supersessionism can cover a multitude of perspectives about the church vis-à-vis the Jews—i.e., antiquation, representation, replacement, supplement, succession, superiority, superordination, etc.—then it is so broad as to be baseless as a criticism. Supersessionism, then, sadly amounts

---

6. Scot McKnight, "Saints Re-formed: The Extension and Expansion of *Hagios* in Paul," in *One God, One People, One Future: Essays in Honour of N. T. Wright*, ed. J. A. Dunne and E. Lewellen (London: SPCK, 2018), 211.

7. Bruce Marshall, "Christ and the Cultures: The Jewish People and Christian Theology," in *The Cambridge Companion to Christian Doctrine*, ed. Colin Gunton (Cambridge: Cambridge University Press, 1997), 82.

8. See, for example, David Novak, "The Covenant in Rabbinic Thought," in *Two Faiths, One Covenant? Jewish and Christian Identity in the Presence of the Other*, ed. Eugene B. Korn and John T. Pawlikowski (Lanham, MD: Sheed & Ward, 2005), 65–67; J. Brian Tucker, *Reading Romans after Supersessionism: The Continuation of Jewish Covenantal Identity* (Eugene, OR: Wipf & Stock, 2018), 65–80.

9. R. Kendall Soulen, *The God of Israel and Christian Theology* (Minneapolis: Fortress, 1996), 25–32; R. Kendall Soulen, "The Standard Canonical Narrative and the Problem of Supersessionism," in *Introduction to Messianic Judaism: Its Ecclesial Context and Biblical Foundations*, ed. David Rudolph and Joel Willitts (Grand Rapids: Zondervan, 2013), 282–91; followed by Steven D. Aguzzi, *Israel, the Church, and Millenarianism: A Way Beyond Replacement Theology* (London: Routledge, 2018), 24–29.

10. Wright, *Paul and the Faithfulness of God*, 806.

to nothing more than a mode of scholarly, in-house, deviant-labeling against any interpreter daring to articulate a perspective on Paul that is not sufficiently conducive to some preferred vision of interfaith relationships. Supersessionism is not a single thing; rather, it is a family of views about Paul and the Jews that some scholars believe requires decontamination from their discourse.

Just to be clear, that is not to say that Paul doesn't sometimes write things about the Jews that are jarring and make us cringe (e.g., 1 Thess 2:14–16). Nor is it the case that there are readings of Paul, Israel, and the Jews that veer into anti-Semitism and a disparagement of Israel that should be earnestly resisted for their accuracy as well as their application. Nor does it mean that we should not pursue a responsible appropriation of Paul for our own multifaith, global world. What Paul said is one thing; what we choose to do with it is quite another!

My point is that merely raising the spectre of supersessionism does not amount to a critique except in an ad hominem sense within certain scholarly environs where supersessionism operates as a form of deviant-labeling. That is because supersession is not a single view; rather, it is a spectrum of views, and each one is different from the other.

SUPERSESSIONISM IS JEWISH

A further consideration we need to explore is that supersessionism is a distinctively intra-Jewish phenomenon. In the sectarian context of Second Temple Judaism, various Judean and diasporan groups clashed over who are the authentic heirs of Israel's religious heritage, who speaks for God, who belongs to God, and who will be saved by God in an eschatological deliverance. These groups engaged in ferocious denunciations of each other, while simultaneously presaging their own claims for a privileged position before God.

The Qumran community identified itself with salient terms such as "sons of light" (1QM 1.1), "people of God" (1QM 1.5), "sons of righteousness" (1QM 1.8), the "diggers at the well" (CD 4.11), the "congregation of God" (1QS 1.12), those to whom "shall belong all the glory

of Adam" (1QS 4.22–23), "the house of truth in Israel" (1QS 5.6; 8.9),
and "a temple for Israel" (1QS 8.5). It is hard to establish a consistent picture of the sect in relation to other Judean groups, given that
the literature is varied and defies systematization into anything like
an ecclesiology. Debate pertains to whether the Qumran sectarians
regarded themselves as a "true Israel," a "remnant," or as something
like the representatives of Israel in the messianic age.[11] The sect certainly regarded itself as elect over and against the gentiles, Jewish
apostates, or even lax Jews outside the sect. Consequently, it could
discursively describe itself as the "Israel" who has volunteered to
become a community of the "covenant" (1QS 5.22) and the "congregation of Israel in the last days" (1QSa 1.2). Qumran's halakhic development, worship, pesher interpretation, Yahad self-conception, and
sectarian polemics[12] make it hard not to associate it with some mode
of intra-Jewish sectarian supersessionism.[13]

---

11. Contrast W. D. Davies, "The Dead Sea Scrolls and Christian Origins," in
Christian Origins and Judaism (London: Darton, Longman & Todd, 1962), 102;
Sanders, *Paul and Palestinian Judaism*, 245–47; Graham Harvey, *The True Israel:
Uses of the Names Jew, Hebrew and Israel in Ancient Jewish Literature and Early
Christian Literature*, AGAJU 35 (Leiden: Brill, 1996), 217; Markus Bockmuehl,
"1QS and Salvation at Qumran," in *The Complexities of Second Temple Judaism, vol.
1 of Justification and Variegated Nomism*, ed. D. A. Carson, Peter T. O'Brien, and
M. A. Seifrid (Grand Rapids: Baker, 2001), 388–94; Sigurd Grindheim, *The Crux of
Election*, WUNT 2.202 (Tübingen: Mohr/Siebeck, 2005), 67–69; Wright, *Paul and
the Faithfulness of God*, 809–10.

12. My thoughts here are stimulated by an email conversation with Markus
Bockmuehl (5 Oct 2019).

13. Note too Daniel C. Harlow's comparison of Paul with Qumran on election:
"Disagreement over who is elect was certainly part of intra-Jewish debate in the
Second Temple period. This is clear enough from the sectarian Dead Sea Scrolls.
Paul, however went a step beyond the covenanters at Qumran: for them not all Jews
are elect, but all the elect are still Jews. Not so for Paul: only those in Christ are in
the covenant and among the elect. In his vision of a new humanity destined for a
new creation, ethnicity—so essential to Jewish identity—disappears. If this theology
implies no wholesale rejection or supersession of Israel, it does imply a new definition of 'Israel' and a displacement of historic Israel's covenantal self-understanding as
a community formed by physical descent and ritual observance" (Daniel C. Harlow,

The Enochic writings are replete with language of election and sectarian boundary-erection. Within the Similitudes, the "congregation of the righteous" (1 En 38.1) constitute "the holy, the righteous, and the elect" (38.4; 48.1) over against "sinners" and the "wicked" (38.3) and the "kings of the earth and the mighty landowners" (48.8). The "elect" cling "onto the Lord of Spirits" (40.5) in contrast to the "sinners" who "deny the name of the Lord of the Spirits" (45.1–2). In 1 Enoch's Animal Apocalypse, the elect are represented by white cows and white sheep (85.3, 8; 89.1, 9, 12–27; 90.6–36) whereas the nonelect are represented by a wild ass and a black boar (89.11–12). Blindness is used as a metaphor for disobedience to the law, while obedience to the law is the sign of election. In the narration, some sheep have had their eyes pecked out (90.2), some sheep have made themselves blind (89.54), some sheep begin to open their eyes during the time of Moses (89.28), and at the consummation all the sheep have their eyes opened (90.35). The Enochic narrative concentrates election in a particular law-observant group within Israel.[14] Then, in the Apocalypse of Weeks, a distinction is drawn between, on the one hand, "sinners" and, on the other hand, the "righteous," "children of righteousness," "elect ones of the world," and "elect ones of righteousness" (91.12; 93.1, 10). In particular, a distinction is made within "the eternal plant of righteousness," which symbolizes Israel, between "an apostate generation" of the seventh week and "the elect ones of righteousness" who succeed them in an eighth week (93.9–10). The election of the elect transpires during the seventh week, amid a time of crisis and judgment, resulting in the deliverance of the author's community. Overall, across 1 Enoch we are confronted by intra-group differentiation, prestige labels, sectarian rivalries, and denunciations that espouse the eschatological fitness of a "true Israel."[15]

"Early Judaism and Early Christianity," in *Early Judaism: A Comprehensive Overview*, ed. John J. Collins and Daniel C. Harlow [Grand Rapids: Eerdmans, 2012], 405).

14. Grindheim, *Crux of Election*, 43.

15. E. P. Sanders, *Paul and Palestinian Judaism* (Philadelphia: Fortress, 1977), 361.

Coming to Philo, he uses a peculiar designation of the "Israel who sees God" (Ἰσραήλ ὅς ἐστι θεὸν ὁρῶν).[16] According to Jacob Neusner, for Philo, "Israel" is a cluster of philosophical commitments, a certain perception of God, rendering Israel as an intellectual rather than ethnic category.[17] Ellen Birnbaum suggests that "seeing God represents the height of human happiness and that, in and of itself, seeing God may be considered universal since anyone—regardless of birth—may pursue this quest or goal."[18] Given that Philo normally distinguishes Israel from the Jewish people, Birnbaum infers: "accordingly, 'Israel' is not a clearly recognizable social group but instead may be similar to what we speak of today as an 'intellectual elite.'"[19] The result is that "Israel" for Philo is shorn its ethnographical traits and designates any philosophically minded and ethically upright monotheist irrespective as to whether they are Jews or not.[20] Although one joins the Jewish people by adopting certain customs, one strives to belong to Israel by philosophical reflection.[21] Philo's "Israel" might not be technically supersessionist, but it is certainly elitist and construes belonging to God in categories beyond Jewish genealogy, ethnicity, and cultus.

If Paul's abrupt remarks about Jews and Torah as well as the prestige labels he applies to his gentile assemblies are placed beside the sectarian semantics of the Qumran scrolls, Enochic literature, and Philo, then, as Jon D. Levenson, observed, "the longstanding claim of the Church that it supersedes the Jews, in large measure continues the old narrative pattern in which a late-born son dislodges his first-born brothers, with varying degrees of success. Nowhere does Christianity

---

16. Philo, *Migr. Abr.* 113–14; *Conf. Ling.* 56; *Rer. Div. Her.* 78.

17. Jacob Neusner, *Judaism and Its Social Metaphors: Israel in the History of Jewish Thought* (Cambridge: Cambridge University Press, 1989), 221.

18. Ellen Birnbaum, *The Place of Judaism in Philo's Thought: Israel, Jews and Proselytes* (Providence: Brown University Press, 1996), 11.

19. Birnbaum, *Place of Judaism*, 12.

20. Birnbaum, *Place of Judaism*, 115–16.

21. Birnbaum, *Place of Judaism*, 212–13.

betray its indebtedness to Judaism more than in its supersessionism."[22] Wright explains that further:

> In other words, Judaism has always contained a narrative pattern in which a late-born son supplants older brothers, or a new movement (such as Qumran) claims to represent or embody the true people of God. One could even regard the Mishnah as 'supersessionist,' since it sketches a way of being Jewish which many Jews of earlier generations would neither have recognised nor approved.[23]

This is the meaning of Paul's "sectarian supersessionism," as Wright calls it.[24] If one contends that all supersessionism per se is anti-Jewish, a product of prejudice and malice, then whole swaths of Jewish literature, not just Paul, would need to be similarly characterized—a frankly incomprehensible conclusion, itself indicating that something has gone amiss in the domain of supersessionist studies.[25]

Paul's supersessionism is inherited from his Jewish framework, worked out in a messianic matrix which itself draws heavily on the

---

22. Jon D. Levenson, *The Death and Resurrection of the Beloved Son: The Transformation of Child Sacrifice in Judaism and Christianity* (New Haven: Yale University Press, 1995), x, affirmed by Wright, *Paul and the Faithfulness of God*, 809 n110. See also Joel Kaminsky and Mark Reasoner who comment: "Any Christian reading of the Hebrew Scriptures is likely to involve some form of supersessionism, by which we mean that the early Christians came to believe that their reading of Israel's scriptures superseded other earlier and contemporary readings of these sacred texts by other Jewish readers and that God's acting through Jesus's death and resurrection had ushered in the beginning of the eschaton, thus opening a path for gentiles to participate in God's promises to Israel" (Joel Kaminsky and Mark Reasoner, "The Meaning and Telos of Israel's Election: An Interfaith Response to N. T. Wright's Reading of Paul," *HTR* 112.4 [2019]: 422n2).

23. Wright, *Paul and the Faithfulness of God*, 809.

24. Wright, *Paul and the Faithfulness of God*, 806–10.

25. Bruce Longenecker, "On Israel's God and God's Israel: Assessing Supersessionism in Paul," *JTS* 58 (2007): 40.

Jewish scriptures, and was asserted in the fractious socioreligious context of the eastern Mediterranean diaspora.

SUPERSESSIONISM AS INEVITABLE

To be brutally honest, supersessionism is simply unavoidable if we are engaging in a close and contextual reading of Paul within Judaism. When one expounds Paul's penetrating statements about the Torah and sin, salvation through Christ and not through the Torah, Jewish antagonism toward the gospel, and the place of gentiles as members God's people without becoming proselytes to Judaism, then supersessionism is simply inescapable. The only questions are "What type of supersessionism will be identified?" and "What will one do with it?"

One of the oldest and, yes, most pernicious supersessionist readings of Paul is that found in classic Protestantism: the Jews rejected Christ; they clung to the law and spurned the gospel; therefore Paul announced them as eternally rejected by God and henceforth replaced by the gentile church. As Soulen describes it, "God abrogates God's covenant with Israel ... on account of Israel's rejection of Christ and the gospel."[26] The result is the view that Adolf Harnack expressed: "The Jewish nation in which Jesus Christ appeared, has, for the time at least, no special relation to the God whom Jesus revealed."[27] That view is, I would argue, demonstrably un-Pauline.

Or else, in far more benign terms, as E. P. Sanders famously said, "in short, this is what Paul finds wrong in Judaism: it is not Christianity."[28] While that might constitute an innocuous and banal statement, it is based on Sanders's observation that "Paul in fact explicitly denies that the Jewish covenant can be effective for salvation."[29] Further, Sanders maintained that Paul regarded his assemblies

---

26. Soulen, *God of Israel and Christian Theology*, 30.

27. Adolf von Harnack, *Outlines of the History of Dogma*, trans. E. K. Mitchell (1893; repr., Eugene, OR: Wipf & Stock, 2001), 42.

28. Sanders, *Paul and Palestinian Judaism*, 552.

29. Sanders, *Paul and Palestinian Judaism*, 551.

as effectively a third race, neither Jewish nor gentile, but rather a new eschatological and transethnic entity. The third-race ecclesiology is strongly rejected by anti-supersessionist advocates.[30] Yet Sanders asserts that "Paul's view of the church, supported by his practice, against his own conscious intention was substantially that it was a third entity, not just because it was composed of both Jew and Greek, but also because it was in important ways neither Jewish nor Greek."[31] In the mind of Paul, according to Sanders, God has done a new thing in Christ; this new thing saves and is not available in Judaism as it is commonly practiced; it creates a new people who are neither Jewish nor gentiles; and Paul grieves that some Jews are despising it. I submit that Sanders, for all his sensitivities and nuances, finds a form of supersessionism in Paul.

Even among those in the Paul-within-Judaism school or who hold to a "two ways" of salvation for gentiles (in Christ) and for Jews (in their covenant), there is still a tacit deficiency in the Jewish disposition that is corrected by Paul's testimony. Lloyd Gaston said, "This is what Paul finds wrong with other Jews: that they do not share his revelation in Damascus."[32] Gaston insinuates that the Jews, by failing to see Christ as the instrument for incorporating gentiles into Israel's ancestral faith, either as guests or as equals, have spurned God's inclusive act toward gentiles in Christ. Paul's Jewish compatriots have therefore reinforced a cultic-ethnic barrier that inhibited Jewish-gentile relationships within a common faith. That view is either superseded or revised by Paul's messianic faith, which draws gentiles into the Jewish constituency. This too is supersessionism, because

---

30. Lionel J. Windsor, *Reading Ephesians and Colossians after Supersessionism: Christ's Mission through Israel to the Nations* (Eugene, OR: Cascade, 2017), 41–46.

31. E. P. Sanders, *Paul, the Law, and the Jewish People* (Philadelphia: Fortress, 1983), 178; cf. Bird, *An Anomalous Jew*, 49–57; Wright, *Paul and the Faithfulness of God*, 1443–49.

32. Lloyd Gaston, *Paul and the Torah* (Vancouver: University of British Columbia Press, 1987), 140.

Paul believed in the superiority of his inclusive view over the exclusive view of his compatriots.

Consequently, Paul's discourse about Christ and Torah as well as Christ-believers in proximity to non-Christ-believing Jews will inevitably drive us toward identifying his position with some species of supersessionism; it is a matter of what kind we detect and how we describe it.

PAULINE SUPERSESSIONISM:
AN EXPOSITION

Paul's discourses in Galatians 1–4, 2 Corinthians 3, and Romans 1–4 and 9–11 express a range of continuities and discontinuities between Judaism and Christ-faith. All in all, Paul regarded the covenantal architecture of Israel's ancestral religion, as expressed in common Judaism, as formative yet fulfilled (to put it positively) or deficient and defunct (to put it negatively). Paul, whether engaged in polemics or pastoral persuasion, often makes nakedly provocative statements that are rooted in common Judaism, yet he proceeds to redefine Jewish nodes of identity, praxis, and community boundaries in ways that grate against common Judaism. Paul declares:

> The sting of death is sin, and the power of sin is the Torah. (1 Cor 15:56)[33]

> If righteousness comes through the Torah, then Christ died for nothing. (Gal 2:21)

> But Torah came in, with the result that the trespass multiplied; but where sin increased, grace abounded all the more, so that, just as sin exercised dominion in death, so grace might also exercise dominion through justification leading to eternal life through Jesus Christ our Lord. (Rom 5:20–21)

---

33. Scripture quotations in this essay are the author's translation.

God has done what the Torah, weakened by the flesh, could
not do: by sending his own Son in the likeness of sinful flesh,
and to deal with sin, he condemned sin in the flesh, so that
the just requirement of the Torah might be fulfilled in us, who
walk not according to the flesh but according to the Spirit.
(Rom 8:3–4).

These remarks are rooted in Jewish discourse, but they carve out
an unprecedented path within it. Paul's anthropological pessimism
meant he identified a problem with humanity, among both Jews and
gentiles, that Israel's covenant and Torah could not fix. As Bruce
Longenecker comments, "in the face of the cosmic powers of Sin and
Death," Paul "considered the solely theocentric faith of mainstream
forms of Judaism to be underdeveloped, unenlightened, and salvifi-
cally deficient, and therein lies his supersessionism."[34]

A comparison of Paul and Rabbi Akiba is illuminating. When
Rabbi Akiva declared Simon Bar Kochbar to be the Messiah, there
was no way that Israel could simply go about its normal business. If
Bar Kochbar was the Messiah, then everything changed or had to be
changed; new tasks emerged, a new temple had to be built, new coins
had to be minted, new relaxations and intensifications of Torah were
required, and a war had to be fought. In fact, the rabbinic Judaism of
the post-135 CE era can regarded as a type of supersessionism of the
earlier varieties of Judaism that preceded it. The same was true of Paul,
for whom a new symbolic universe and a redefinition of Israel was
born from his messianic eschatology. Consequently, Wright is surely
correct in his Pauline supersessionism in the sense that if the Messiah
has come, if Israel's Messiah has indeed been crucified-raised-exalted,
if gentiles were worshiping God for his mercy through the Messiah
and in the Spirit, and if a new age has dawned and awaits an apocalyptic denouement, "then it is impossible to imagine [Paul], or any
second-temple Jew in a comparable position, supposing that this

---

34. Longenecker, "On Israel's God," 34–35, 39.

Messiah could have his followers while 'Israel' could carry on as though nothing had happened."[35]

In addition, Paul effectively dissolved the in-between position of God-fearer (θεοσεβής)—a gentile adherent to Jewish ways, who is attached to and active among a Jewish community but is not formally admitted to the Jewish community (Rom 4; Gal 3–4). This was not unprecedented within Judaism, since Philo and Josephus narrate many examples of Jews who wanted to attract and even incorporate non-Jews into Jewish assemblies without the males having to undergo the physically harsh and socially expensive cost of circumcision. But the rationale for Paul's dissolution of the of-but-not-in category was not social expedience, but election, eschatology, and experience! For Paul, Jews and gentiles are equal "in Christ" by faith and the Spirit (Gal 3:5, 28; 4:6); otherwise, God would be the God of the Jews only (Rom 3:29). Circumcision is nullified (1 Cor 7:19; Gal 5:6; 6:15) and reinterpreted (Rom 2:25–29; Phil 3:3) as a marker of belongingness to God's people. The operating premise is that Abraham is the ancestor of *all* who believe in Christ, and Paul wants Jews and gentiles alike to "walk in the footsteps of the foreskinned faith of our forefather Abraham" (Rom 4:12). He further describes his ethnically mixed congregations with language such as "elect" (Rom 8:33) and "chosen" (1 Thess 1:4), drawn from scriptural designations for Israel (e.g. Ps 104:6; Isa 43:20; 45:4 LXX). These Christ-believing groups are neither Jews nor pagans but rather the "assembly of God," a prestigious group with a privileged relationship with Israel's God through Christ (1 Cor 10:32). Scripture is written for them (Rom 4:23–25) and even about them, because they are the ones "on whom the ends of the ages have come" (1 Cor 10:11). Taken together, this is not the language of

---

35. Wright, *Paul and the Faithfulness of God*, 985–86. Wright also points out: "The scandal of Paul's gospel, after all, was that the events in which he claimed that Israel's God had been true to what he promised centred on a crucified Messiah. That is the real problem with any and all use of the 'supersession' language: either Jesus was and is Israel's Messiah, or he was not and is not" (810).

replacement, but the introduction of a "mutation" of Jewish identity to include Christ-believing gentiles within it.[36] The question becomes therefore, how do gentile Christ-believers in an expansive Israel relate to unbelieving Jews who are ostensibly part of ethnic Israel? The answer, of course, is Paul's discourse in Romans 9–11, and this too will find us wrestling with a type of supersessionism.

Whereas some Jewish groups conceived of themselves as an elect within Israel (Jews superseding other Jews in a salvific-eschatological narrative), Paul's discourse is different. For Paul, the advent of the Messiah has created a fissure within ethnic Israel between those who believe and those who do not, between an Israel according to the flesh and an Israel according to the promise (Rom 9:6–21). For the promissory Israel, they comprise a remnant of Christ-believing Jews (9:27–29; 11:1–5) and gentile Christ-believers who are grafted into promissory Israel's election by faith (9:22–26; 10:4–13; 11:20, 24). For Paul, "Israel" is a prestige label for the superordinate group comprised of Christ-believing Jews and gentiles, who can be described elsewhere as an "inward Jew" (Rom 2:29), "children of the living God" (Rom 9:26), the "circumcision" (Phil 3:3), and the "Israel of God" (Gal 6:16). This leaves ethnic Israel in an ambiguous space. On the one hand, they are objects of "wrath" (Rom 9:22) because they "stumbled" (9:32–33; 11:11–12), committed a "transgression" (11:11–12), are "defeated" (11:12), have become "a disobedient and obstinate people" (10:21; 11:30–31), have been "hardened" (9:18; 11:7, 25), experienced "rejection" (11:15), were "broken off because of unbelief" (11:20), and have become "enemies" of God (11:28). But on the other hand, Paul simultaneously affirms that God has "not rejected his people" (11:1–2), Israel is not beyond recovery (11:11), God's love for Israel is immutable (11:28), and Israel's election is "irrevocable" (11:29).

---

36. Cf. John M. G. Barclay, *Jews in the Mediterranean Diaspora: From Alexander to Trajan (323 BCE–117 CE)* (Edinburgh: T&T Clark, 1996), 395; Ellis Rivkin, "Paul's Jewish Odyssey," *Judaism* (1989): 233.

The tension here is real, and Paul intensifies it further. He does that, first, by ruling out a replacement view of Israel, attacking the thesis that the "branches were broken off *so that* I might be grafted in" (Rom 11:19, italics added). Then, second, Paul has no place for a *sonderweg* where Israel is saved under the auspices of an existing Mosaic scheme without Christ. Israel can and will be saved, but with a note of christological conditionality: "if they do not persist in unbelief" (11:23). The dilemma is not whether Israel is elect, but how Israel's election and disobedience to the gospel will be resolved and how she relates to Christ-believing Jews and gentiles.

The relationship of Christ-believing gentiles to non-Christ-believing Jews is not one of superiority. How could it be? The Jews still have "advantages" (περισσός; Rom 3:1) and an enviable list of privileges, including a genealogical relationship to the patriarchs and the Messiah (Rom 9:4–5). Importantly, the relationship between Christ-believing gentiles and non-Christ-believing Jews is not competitive, but an interlocking destiny (Rom 11:17–20, 28–31; cf. 1:16; 2:9–10; 15:8–9). We see that in two ways.

First, gentile deliverance is nourished by its Jewish roots (Rom 11:16–18), and gentiles are saved only by being grafted into Israel's election (11:17). For Paul, in God's purposes, Israel's misstep over the Messiah was tragic yet necessary, as it occasioned "riches for the world" (11:12) and brought "reconciliation to the world" (11:15). Israel's disbelief and disobedience led to gentile inclusion (11:11, 31). Israel's gospel failure is "for" the benefit of the gentiles as much as Israel's election is "for" the benefit of bringing to fruition the patriarchal promises about many nations worshiping God (11:28; cf. 15:7–8)— in which case Israel's election, covenantal privileges, and even her stumbling are the instruments for gentile deliverance, making Israel intrinsic to gentile salvation. Israel might be disobedient and might disparage members of Christ's body, but she remains indispensable to God's purposes. Thus, with Longenecker again: "Paul imagined ethnic Israel, whether hardened or enlivened, to play the role of God's specially chosen instrument in the course of salvation history. And

in this Paul sees the intransience of God's covenant with the Jews."[37]
Thus, we reach an important judgment: *extra Israel nulla salus*, "outside of Israel there is no salvation."[38]

Second, the church is the agent of Israel's deliverance, too. For, much like Qumran's "eternal planting" on behalf of Israel (1QS 8.5; 1.7–9; Jub 16.26), Paul envisages the church as the shoot from the tree stump of Jesse from which the whole tree would be renewed and sprout forth again.[39] Paul's conviction is that the natural Jewish branch belongs in the olive tree (Rom 11:24), even if it was broken off *momentarily* for unbelief (11:20, 23), and Israel's "hardening" is only *temporary* until the "fullness of the gentiles has come in" (11:25). Paul hopes that the gentile worship of God will prompt ethnic Israel to "jealousy" (11:11, 14), so that ethnic Israel can be grafted back into God's purposes (11:23–24). Such a vision justifies the continued mission of proclamation to ethnic Israel (10:1, 14–15; 11:14), so that she can be "saved" in the present time (10:13; 11:14), or in an eschatological consummation (11:26). The gospel remains for the Jew first and then the Greek (1:16), not for the Greek instead of the Jew![40] God's purposes for ethnic Israel in the end are their "fullness" (πλήρωμα; 11:12), "acceptance" (πρόσλημψις; 11:15), and "forgiveness" (11:27; cf. Isa 27:9; Jer 31:34). Thus, God's mercy may appear capricious (Rom 9:15–16, 18, 23), but it proves in the end to be comprehensive, since

37. Longenecker, "Assessing Supersessionism," 39.

38. See Bird, *An Anomalous Jew*, 118–19; Dale B. Martin, "The Promise of Teleology, the Constraints of Epistemology, and the Universal Vision of Paul," in *St. Paul among the Philosophers*, ed. John D. Caputo and Linda Martín Alcoff (Bloomington: Indiana University Press, 2009), 101: "The theme of Romans, put in Latin, would not be *extra ecclesiam nulla salus* (no salvation outside of the church), but, and this is what so many Christians refuse to recognize when they read Romans, *extra Israel nulla salus*: 'there is no salvation outside of Israel.'"

39. I owe this point to an email conversation with Markus Bockmuehl (5 Oct 2019).

40. D. Kaylor, *Paul's Covenant Community: Jew and Gentile in Romans* (Atlanta: John Knox, 1988), 159.

God's electing mercy for promissory Israel (9:6–29) will eschatologically encompass even ethnic Israel (11:30–32). That is the "mystery"
of which he speaks (11:25).

I submit that, according to Paul, the singularity of salvation in Christ
and the giving of the Spirit to non-Jews entailed a deficit in the Mosaic
dispensation, the secondment of the Torah in the service of sin and
death, the inability of the Torah to save and define God's people, Israel's
stumbling for its rejection of Christ and clinging to the Torah for righteousness, and the expansion of Israel to include non-Jews. This is
a distinctly Pauline account, but is also at the heart of Christianity.
McKnight points out that, "at some level, according to many, any firm
conviction that Jesus is the world's savior, including the savior for Jews,
is supersessionism."[41] The only alternative McKnight adds is "religious
pluralism," in which case Christian faith, so long as it sees in Christ a
revelation of something that was not otherwise available, makes supersessionism intrinsic to its narrative fixtures. According to David Novak:

> It seems to me that Christianity must be generically super-
> sessionist. In fact, I question the Christian orthodoxy of any
> Christian who claims he or she is not a supersessionist at all.
> The reason for my suspicion is as follows: If Christianity did
> not come into the world to bring something better than what
> Judaism did not or could not bring itself, then why shouldn't
> anyone who wants a concrete relationship with the God of
> Abraham, Isaac, and Jacob—and their descendants—either
> remain within normative Judaism or convert to it? ... And,
> the Jews have been accepting converts long before the Church
> came to be, so no one need look to Christianity as a Judaism
> for the gentiles. The gentiles can get their Judaism straight
> from the Jews. As such, Christians must believe that they are

---

41. Scot McKnight, "The New Perspective and the Christian Life: The Ecclesial
Life," in *The Apostle Paul and the Christian Life: Ethical and Missional Implications of
the New Perspective,* ed. Scot McKnight and Joseph B. Modica (Grand Rapids: Baker,
2016), 133.

offering the world something better or else why not remain Jews or become Jews?"[42]

There is, then, no *after* or *beyond* supersessionism for Paul or for any other Christian author. That is because Paul is inevitably supersessionist due to his messianic eschatology: salvation and consummation are revealed in Christ and nowhere else.[43]

CONCLUSION

In this essay I have argued that: (1) there are several species of supersessionism, so to use "supersessionism" as a pejorative jibe in scholarship is disingenuous; (2) supersessionism is part and parcel of Jewish sectarianism as to whose way of being Israel should avail, and Paul is an inheritor of that tradition; (3) supersessionism is inescapable in Paul's perspective, given that he detects something deficient among his Jewish contemporaries regarding either the instrument or scope of salvation; and (4) Paul's messianic eschatology leads to viewing Israel as not replaced but expanded to include Christ-believing gentiles, so that Paul can simultaneously affirm that the distinction between Jews and gentiles is negated even as he retains a place for ethnic Israel in God's purposes.

If the preceding analysis is true, if Paul is supersessionist in the sense described above, the question is: What shall we do with it? According to two Dutch theologians, Cornelis van der Kooi and Gijsberg van den Brink, Israel is the "raw nerve in Christian theology."[44] The history of Christian vitriol and violence against the Jews will forever cast a shadow over the church's past, present, and future relationship with Jewish communities around the world. We cannot help but read Paul—as well as Matthew, John, Ignatius, Chrysostom,

---

42. Novak, "Covenant in Rabbinic Thought," 67.

43. See similarly Wright, *Paul and the Faithfulness of God*, 1412n10.

44. Cornelis van der Kooi and Gijsberg van den Brink, *Christian Dogmatics: An Introduction*, trans. Reinder Bruinsma with James D. Bratt (Grand Rapids: Eerdmans, 2017), 338.

Luther, and Barth—except in light of the horror of Shoah, and we
must read responsibly. We can ask: Would Paul have written what
he did in Romans 9–11, Galatians 4, and 1 Thessalonians 2:14–16 if
he knew the history we knew? Should we follow Paul given that we
know where this all led? Should we not burn and bury every instance
of supersessionism for its christological dogmatism? The challenge for
Christians is to simultaneously affirm the *solus Christus* of their confession (Christ alone is Savior) and the proposition that *extra Israel
nulla salus* (outside of Israel there is no salvation) without denigrating
those who share in the flesh and family of the Jewish Messiah. Jesus is
and always will be a "servant of the Jews" (Rom 15:8), and the Jewish
"no" to Jesus must be comprehended in light of God's "yes" to all
people (2 Cor 1:18–20), especially his intended "acceptance" of Israel
and "mercy" for Israel through Christ (Rom 11:15, 31). As such: "The
church does not take the place of Israel but sees itself as a community
that is privileged to share in the expectation that was given to Israel."[45]

---

45. Van der Kooi and van den Brink, *Christian Dogmatics*, 342.

PAUL, GALATIANS, AND SUPERSESSIONISM

BEN WITHERINGTON III

"The Epistle to the Galatians is my Epistle: I have
betrothed myself to it; it is my wife."

—Martin Luther

"Luther speaks as Paul would have spoken had he
lived at the time when Luther gave his lectures."

—Hans Dieter Betz[1]

To say that Galatians is a controversial discourse that has
prompted heated reactions over many centuries is to say too
little. Galatians is the dynamite that Luther used to blow up
all sorts of extant notions on what counted as genuine Christian belief
and praxis in his own era, thereby helping to launch the Protestant
Reformation. And so it is not too much to say that the Paul-within-
Judaism point of view has had a very hard time fitting Galatians into
their larger argument that Paul lived out his religious life within his
native Judaism, and was not the creator of the "partings of the ways"

---

1. Both of these quotes can be found in H. D. Betz, *Galatians: A Commentary on
Paul's Letter to the Churches in Galatia*, (Philadelphia: Fortress, 1979), xv.

between early Judaism and the Christ movement.[2] Indeed, in reviewing Paula Fredriksen's book *Paul: The Pagans' Apostle*, I have even said the following:

> The attempt to tame Paul and make him still fit into early Jewish shoes of an ordinary sort only with a Messianic logo on them rather than a Nike swoosh, was rightly warned against by two of the best Jewish scholars in our field—both A. Segal and D. Boyarin. Paul was indeed a radical Jew, one who would not and will not be neatly fit even into the surprising diversity of early Judaism as it existed before Christ. He believed of course that the Hebrew Bible was the Word of God, that Jesus was both the Jewish messiah and the savior of gentiles, he believed the Scriptures were being fulfilled and the eschatological dreams of Isaiah and others were coming to pass. He also believed that God had given Israel covenants plural (Rom. 9.1–5) not just a single covenant renewed again and again. He saw the new covenant as the fulfillment of the Abrahamic covenant, and the Mosaic covenant as a temporary covenant meant to keep God's people in line until the Messiah came (Gal. 4.1ff). This was not the view of *all* the earliest Jewish followers of Christ, as the example of the circumcision party in Galatia makes clear, but it was certainly Paul's view. If neither circumcision nor uncircumcision counts but rather only new creation, if it is true of anyone who is in Christ, Jew or gentile, then Paul is not merely saying in 1 Cor. 7 circumcision doesn't matter for gentile converts to Christ. No, he is saying since there is a new covenant which does not require that of

---

2. See, for example, Paula Fredriksen's recent important book *Paul: The Pagans' Apostle* (New Haven: Yale University Press, 2017), where one of the main givens of her argument is that Paul remained within his native Judaism throughout his life, and this despite the protests of A. Segal and D. Boyarin that Paul was quite rightly viewed by many fellow Jews as clearly having committed apostasy from Judaism, even taking into account the broad spectrum of Jewish beliefs and varied praxis in his day.

anyone, it simply doesn't matter in light of the new eschatological situation. The Mosaic covenant though holy and good
has had its day, and is fading into obsolescence in light of the
new covenant and the glory of Christ. Paul's mission was not
law or commandment free, it was Mosaic covenant free. There
were still commandments aplenty in the new covenant, some
of which derived from the previous contract/covenant.[3]

Further discussion of the matter is required, not least because
the Paul-within-Judaism movement has gained more adherents and
momentum in the last ten or so years, but also because all sorts of
publications have been supporting such a reading of Paul. In the
first major part of this essay, I want to interact with some of the
detailed critiques by John Barclay of that kind of reading of Paul,
and especially of Galatians; then, in the second half of the essay,
I want to turn to some of the more exegetical points that make it
impossible to fit Galatians into that sort of worldview or paradigm.
Finally, we will address directly whether Paul should be charged with
"supersessionism."

JOHN BARCLAY ON
PAUL-WITHIN-JUDAISM

No one could accuse John Barclay of having not done his homework
in studying the spectrum of views and praxis of early Judaism. Indeed,
he has published one of the finer, more detailed, and more carefully
nuanced critical studies of the world of early Judaism in his *Jews in
the Mediterranean Diaspora*.[4] It is thus all the more important to listen
to his judgments on the flaws of the Paul-within-Judaism argument.
In an important essay, Barclay stresses:

---

3. See my review on my blog: Ben Witherington III, "*Paul: The Pagans' Apostle*, a
Review—Part Eleven," *The Bible and Culture*, 21 February 2018, https://www.patheos.
com/blogs/bibleandculture/2018/02/21/paul-pagans-apostle-review-part-eleven/.

4. John M. G. Barclay, *Jews in the Mediterranean Diaspora: From Alexander to
Trajan (323 BCE–117 CE)* (Edinburgh: T&T Clark, 1996).

I will focus here on Pauline discourse which is unambiguously about kinship, and my aim is to show that in Paul's configuration of this language *his stress lies on a form of identity that is radically contingent on the creative action of God, and thus a type of identity which cannot be mapped onto the ethnic identities claimed or ascribed by human beings. An identity received from God neither enhances ethnic identities nor excludes them.*[5]

What "new creation" *does* do is make those ethnic identities of lesser importance than "being in Christ," and in some sense this new identity transcends and relativizes the older ones. This is seen clearly in Paul's remarkable evaluation of his own personal ethnic identity as a Jew in Philippians 3:3–10. The ethnic identity and the praxis that goes along with it for an observant Jew are seen as worthy of praise, but the point is they pale in significance and are not determinative of belief and behavior in the same way as "being in Christ," growing in Christ, and knowing him and the power of his resurrection. In comparison, Paul is prepared to say he counts his old identity and way of life as *skubala*. This hardly sounds like a person who sees himself as remaining in the Judaism he was formerly a part of—nor, for that matter, does 1 Corinthians 9:20, where Paul indicates he can be the Jew to the Jew. This is a very odd thing for someone ethnically Jewish to say, unless in fact he is no longer chiefly identifying himself in terms of his ethnic Jewishness, but will adopt Jewish praxis for missional reasons—so he might win some Jews to Christ.

Another major point Barclay makes is that it is not enough to suggest that Paul, at least mainly, is writing to gentiles. True enough, but he is not writing just *about gentiles* in Galatians and Romans. For Paul, what he says about salvation while mainly addressing gentiles is nonetheless true for Jews, as well. Barclay puts it this way:

---

5. John M. G. Barclay, "An Identity Received from God: The Theological Configuration of Paul's Kinship Discourse," *Early Christianity* 8 (2017): 354–72, here 356 (italics added).

As is clear in Romans 9–11, it was impossible for Paul to think about Israel's identity except in relation to the gift of God in Christ, and it was impossible to think about the gentile mission except in relation to the destiny of Israel. Paul takes the good news concerning Christ to be for all, "both for the Jew— first—and also for the Greek" (Rom 1:16; 2:9–10; 3:22–23): "For there is no distinction between Jew and Greek: the same Lord is Lord of all, and is rich towards all who call upon him" (Rom 10:12; cf. 1 Cor 1:22–24).

This means that when Paul speaks *to* gentiles (as the primary, implied audience in Galatians and Romans), he must also speak *about* Jews, because the salvation of the whole world is founded on God's mercy to Israel.[6] Where Paul discusses Israel's disobedience (like the prophets, and like other Second Temple Jews), that is not to suggest that Israel's sin is worse than others' but to highlight the power of Sin, which conquers even the best human intentions and frustrates even the best possible Law (Rom 2:17–29; 7:7–25). Such passages have been misused by Christians to suggest that Jews have a supersized sin of arrogance, exclusivity, or self-reliant boasting, but Paul's purpose is to indicate that even the Torah, the greatest defense against Sin, has failed, and that only grace given to the *unrighteous* can match the depth of the human problem. Paul is confident about Israel's future (according to the "mystery" of Rom 11:25–26), not because Israel is unaffected by Sin, but because God has created and sustained Israel by grace and can graft back in those branches that are presently cut off (11:24, 28–32).[7]

---

6. Note the distinction here between the audience (to whom Paul is speaking) and the subject-matter (what he is speaking about).

7. John M. G. Barclay, *Paul and the Power of Grace* (Grand Rapids: Eerdmans, 2020), 146–47 (italics original); this is the lay-friendly version of Barclay's *Paul and the Gift* (Grand Rapids: Eerdmans, 2015). See further, in dialogue with Caroline Johnson-Hodge, John M.G. Barclay, "An Identity Received from God," 354–72.

As we have seen, Israel is—in Paul's view—most truly itself when it trusts in its Messiah, Jesus, and this definitive gift means that Paul places his whole Jewish heritage at the service of, and subordinate to, the ultimate value of "knowing Christ" (Phil 3:4–11). If the Torah can be observed in serving the Lord, Christ, that is good (Rom 14:1–11). But if Torah-observance would destroy the unity among believers or would form a barrier to gentile access to Christ, it would be better for Jews like Peter and Paul to live "in a gentile fashion" (Gal 2:11–14). Speaking as a Jew in Christ (2:15–17), Paul says he has "died to the law" in order to live to God (2:19), because the law is no longer the supreme norm for those whose identity and allegiance have been reconfigured by the gift of Christ (2:19–21).[8] Paul's stance here is subtler than a simple binary choice between comprehensive obedience to the law and utter repudiation of it. Subject to the authority of Christ, Paul can certainly live like a Jew where that serves the purposes of the good news (1 Cor 9:19–23). But because that good news announces a gift given without regard to previous criteria of worth, every cultural tradition (Jewish and non-Jewish) is subject to its supreme criterion of value and every practice made relative to the purposes of Christ.

In the same context, Barclay laments the tendency to oversimplify what is obviously a complex matter—namely, how to calibrate who stands within the spectrum of early Judaism and who does not, given the considerable variety of praxis as well as beliefs in that religion. Is it really true that "statements about 'freedom' from the Jewish Law relate only to Paul's mission to the Gentiles, supporting his insistence that the Law was not to be imposed on them," and that "Paul wanted to bring Gentiles into relation to Israel's God and to Abraham, but in their own Christ-dependent way, distinct from Israel's relationship to God"?[9] Barclay's clear answer, which would be mine as well, is: no, Paul says clearly enough in Galatians that he has died *not* to "law" as a principle (Paul is not combating legalism) or to Roman law as an

---

8. Scripture quotations in this essay are the author's translation.

9. Cited from personal email correspondence with John Barclay.

entity, but quite specifically to the Mosaic law-covenant, which had a good but temporal and temporary function. Nor does Paul affirm a two-track model of salvation—Jews through keeping the Mosaic covenant, gentiles through Christ. No, as Romans 1 says clearly, the good news about Christ is for the Jew first, and also the gentiles. Let us turn now to some of the key details of the rhetorical arguments in Galatians.

ON THE EXEGETICAL MISREADING OF GALATIANS

Despite the best efforts of Mark Nanos and others, few scholars today—even inside the Paul-within-Judaism circles—are prepared to argue that Paul's communities were simply part of the synagogue communities, though there are still a goodly number who affirm Paul spoke purely about gentiles in his remarks about the law in Galatians.[10] While it is true that Paul objects strenuously to the "circumcision" party's attempt to have his gentile converts in Galatia get circumcised and embrace the Mosaic law, this is by no means all he is critiquing in Galatians.

Paul is also very critical of Peter and even Barnabas, two fellow Jewish Christ-followers, for hypocrisy, for "living like a gentile"— which can only mean not living fully in accord with Jewish law and yielding under pressure to the previous praxis (Gal 2). There is a reason Paul calls such behavior *hypocrisy*. It is because he assumes that he and Peter and Barnabas all agree that, even as Jewish followers of Christ, it was not *necessary* to avoid table fellowship with gentiles, not necessary to keep kosher, even as Jews. Under some circumstances, it could be a blessed option—even a missional one to reach more Jews for Christ—but a legal obligation it was not, because the new covenant was not a renewal of the Mosaic one.

---

10. See, however, Mark D. Nanos and Magnus Zetterholm, eds., *Paul within Judaism: Restoring the First-Century Context to the Apostle* (Minneapolis: Fortress, 2015).

Further, the Pauline Gospel involved an inherent critique of the majority of Jews for not recognizing their own Messiah and for failing to realize that the eschatological time had come for one and all to embrace a new covenant inaugurated by Christ's death and resurrection. Peter's hypocrisy was this: while he had affirmed his faith in Christ as the Messiah, and indeed had even entered into a new sort of fellowship with gentile Christ-followers in Antioch, under pressure he went back to his old ways of avoiding "unclean gentiles" and their unclean food. Paul was not simply critiquing Judaizing of gentiles by the circumcision party, though he critiqued that as well. He was criticizing the behavior of his fellow Jewish followers of Jesus for their reversion to previous non-Christ-following behavior.

What of the suggestion that ritual impurity was not that big of a deal, easily remedied by a visit to a *mikveh*, and that eating unclean food was not an earth-shattering thing for a Jew to do? The problem with this suggestion is that it seems all too modern and does not comport with the actual evidence from antiquity, nor does it give enough credence to how early Jews lived in an honor and shame culture, and there was shame attached to violating boundary rituals like eating unclean food. Consider, for example, Peter's recorded reflex reaction to a suggestion he encountered in a dream in Acts 10 that he should eat such food: "absolutely NOT" (Μηδαμῶς, Κύριε; v. 14)!

When one examines the ancient evidence, Peter's reaction seems very much on target—and all too typical. Consider the following Jewish sources: 3 Maccabees 3.4; Josephus, *Against Apion* 2.173–4, 234, 282 (cf. *Ant.* 4.137–39); Letter of Aristeas 139–42. In 4 Maccabees, the refusal to eat pork is so emphatic that Jews are prepared to die instead of doing so (see also Philo, *Leg.* 361–62; *Flacc.* 96). If Jews were ready to die rather than eat such food, it is hardly a matter of "you can get clean afterward." This impression of just how important this matter was in early Judaism is further reinforced by the comments of non-Jews who observed the Jewish praxis of the era as outsiders (Tacitus, *Hist.* 5.5.2; Diodorus 1.1.2; Philostratus, *Life of Apollonius,* 33).[11]

Furthermore, much hinges on understanding Paul's covenantal theology, especially as expressed in Galatians 4, so we must give some detailed consideration of that here and now. In Galatians 4:21–31, Paul is countering the possible arguments *not* of non-Christian Jews but of some fellow Jewish Christians, whom he sees as bewitching his converts in Galatia. This passage contrasts considerably with 1 Thessalonians 2:14–16, where Paul is quite clearly talking about some non-Christian Jews. As Galatians 4 says at the outset, Christ came to redeem those under the Mosaic law out from under that law (4:5). The assumption must be: Paul thinks they needed such redemption.

Put another way, Christ came to inaugurate a new covenant. Paul viewed the Mosaic covenant as an interim solution for God's people, a sort of guardian of them, until Messiah came. He draws an analogy between the Mosaic law and a *paidagogos,* a child minder who supervises a child until they come of age (4:2).[12] The analogy doesn't work if Paul assumed that the Mosaic law covenant should continue to function even after the coming of Christ. And we must bear in mind that Paul has already said in Galatians 2:19 that he himself, a Jew, having been crucified with Christ, had died to that law. It is not surprising, then, that he saw Jewish Christian advocates of the Mosaic law being imposed on *even gentile Christians after* the coming of Christ as being almost as misguided as Hagar when it came to the issue of who was going to inherit the Abrahamic blessings and promises, and how they would do so.

In short, though the Mosaic law had an important function in its day and time, its day and time had come and gone, and that same law

---

11. See Barclay, *Jews in the Mediterranean Diaspora,* 434–37.

12. The fuller form of this argument can be found in Ben Witherington III, *Grace in Galatia* (Edinburgh: T&T Clark, 2000).

(as well as the "time"; 4:4) had been fulfilled by what Christ brought to God's people. In the argument in Galatians 4 then, it is not an accident that Paul tells us that Sarah and Hagar represent *two different covenants*. The story of two women becomes a tale of two covenants in Paul's creative hands. To go back to observing the Mosaic law was tantamount to submitting again to bondage and renouncing the gospel of Christ and the new covenant he instituted. Christians no longer have Jerusalem, or the Mosaic covenant and law, as their mother. Rather: "the Jerusalem which is above is free and she is our mother" (Gal 4:26). I must stress at this juncture that we are dealing with an intramural debate between Paul and other Jewish Christians in regard to how Christians, including gentile Christians, should live. There is no contrast here between Judaism and Christianity. It needs to be said, however, that the view that Paul is *simply* offering teaching that applies *only to gentiles* does not work here or elsewhere.[13]

It is certainly true that Paul sees the new covenant as the fulfillment of the Abraham covenant and the sequel to the Mosaic covenant; he certainly does not see Christianity as replacing Judaism. Indeed, for Paul, being in Christ, the Jewish Messiah, is simply the proper development of the one people of God. The people of God has become Jew and gentile united in the Jewish Messiah. W. D. Davis was right when he said long ago:

> In accepting the Jew, Jesus, as the Messiah, Paul did not think in terms of moving into a new religion but of having found the final expression and intent of the Jewish tradition within which he himself had been born. For him, the Gospel was according to the Scriptures [see e.g. 1 Cor 15:3–5]; it was not an alien importation into Judaism, but the true development of it, its highest point, although in its judgment on the centrality which

---

13. But see Fredriksen, *Paul: The Pagans' Apostle*.

some Jews had given to a particular interpretation of the Law
it showed a radicalism, which amounted to a new creation.[14]

Here a qualification from John Barclay is in order. Paul believes
that Abraham, and indeed all the chosen people of God, are such by
the grace and mercy of God, not due to their ancestry or ethnicity.
After all, Abraham had been a pagan before he "trusted" Yahweh. As
Barclay stresses, it is the mercy and call of God that established and
continues to sustain the people of God, and that is as true since Christ
came as before his time.

Furthermore, Paul is not defending gentile Christianity at the
expense of Jewish Christianity. Rather, as Galatians 3:28 indicates,
he is announcing a true people of God that has come forth as the
true expression of God's saving purposes and that places all persons
on equal footing at the foot of the cross and in the presence of God.
Ethnic distinctions and previous religious customs and rituals are not
given any particular *soteriological significance* in this people of God
united in Christ. When circumcision, Sabbath keeping, food laws, and
other boundary-defining aspects of Judaism are assigned some sort
of salvific status or essential status, Paul opposes such a notion. Paul
has no problems with being the Jew to the Jews in order to win some,
or being the gentile to the gentiles to win some; what he is rejecting is
the necessity of keeping the Mosaic law if one is a Christian. On the
contrary, Christians are called to fulfill a rather different law—"the law
of Christ" (Gal 6:2), which has several components: (1) imitating the
life pattern of Christ; (2) obeying various of the imperatives of Christ,
which Paul reiterates; (3) keeping those Old Testament commandments that have been reiterated by Christ and/or his apostles; and
perhaps (4) obeying the imperatives of the apostles, including Paul's
own, which are viewed as extensions of Christ's teachings.

---

14. W. D. Davis, "Paul and the Gentiles: A Suggestion Concerning Romans 11.13–
24," in *Jewish and Pauline Studies* (Philadelphia: Fortress, 1984), 153–63 (here 160).

Does Paul then call the church Israel? Some have thought so on the basis of Galatians 6:16. Some have contrasted the phrase here ("the Israel *of God*") with the phrase in 1 Corinthians 10:18 that speaks of Israel after the flesh. But context is important in coming to a conclusion at this point. Clearly enough, in Romans 9–11 Paul does use "Israel" to refer to non-Christian Jews. In other words, he is capable of using it in its Old Testament sense. When he says "and in like manner all Israel will be saved" (Rom 11:26), he distinguishes this group of saved persons from the full number of the gentiles who have been grafted into the true people of God.

Galatians 6:16, however, is connected to 6:15, and the entire phrase in question reads: "neither circumcision nor uncircumcision matters; what counts is a new creation. Peace and mercy on all who follow this rule and on the Israel of God." This seems to echo the nineteenth benediction of the Shemoneh Esreh, which reads: "Bestow peace, happiness, and blessing, grace, and loving-kindness, and mercy upon us, and upon all Israel, your people." In Romans 11 as in Galatians there is a distinction of two groups: "us" and "all Israel" in Romans, and "those who keep the rule" and "all Israel" in Galatians. *But,* "the us" in the benediction is a subset of all Jews! And we may suspect that since Paul still views himself and other Jewish Christians as Jews, the "all those who follow this rule" would of course include himself, whom he is perhaps distinguishing from the as-of-yet-not-saved "Israel of God." If that is correct, then even in Galatians 6:16 "the Israel of God" is not a reference to the church.[15]

As Romans 9–11 makes so abundantly clear, Paul agonizes over the fate of Jews who have not, or not yet, accepted their Messiah. He says that he would even be prepared to be cut off from Christ if they could be saved, and in the end, at Romans 11:26 he foresees an eschatological miracle of conversion of Jews to Christ. It is hard to imagine Paul using the term "Israel" to refer either solely or mainly to gentiles who have never yet been a part of Israel. One must bear in mind

---

15. A second but less likely option is that Paul is referring to the Judaizers.

that it is a largely a gentile audience Paul is addressing in Romans, including in Romans 9–11. But who he talks *about* in Romans 9–11 is both gentiles and Jews and their future in Christ. All things considered, then, we may think Paul uses the term "Israel" in Galatians 6:16 as he uses it in Romans, to refer to non-Christian Jews. In any case, the future peace and mercy Paul sees for "the Israel of God" is going to come from Christ, and it is going to come on the same basis as it does for gentiles—through the mercy of God and by means of faith in Jesus Christ.

WAS PAUL A SUPERSESSIONIST?

In many ways, the modern discussion of both early Judaism and early Christianity has suffered from the use of anachronistic terms like "supersessionism," a term Paul would not recognize. Neither would he recognize the notion that the assembly of God in Christ, composed of Jew and gentile alike, should simply be called "Israel" or seen as the sequel or replacement for Israel. No, for Paul, Israel still had a future, but that future was "in Christ." In Romans 11 he explains the mystery of how the full number of gentiles would be saved by grace through faith, by the mercy of God *first*, and then in like manner "all Israel" would be saved by grace through faith in Jesus. When would this happen? When the Redeemer (i.e., Christ) returns from heavenly Zion and turns away the impiety of Jacob, which Paul would never call the *ekklesia tou theou*. In short, the matter was complicated, and the grand union of all the people of God would not transpire before the return of Christ.

Nor would Paul recognize the modern two-track model of salvation—Jews through being true to Torah, gentiles through Jesus. Without question, for Paul, Jesus is both the Messiah for Israel and the Savior of the gentile world. Furthermore, at any one moment in human history since the Christ event, there was only one people of God, with Jew and gentile united in Christ. Paul says Jews who reject Christ are like branches *temporarily* broken off from the tree of God's people, but they can be grafted back in at the eschaton. God has not reneged on his promises to Israel. He can still have mercy even on those who have rejected Jesus of Nazareth, and Paul believes he will do so at the parousia.

The controlling hermeneutical category for Paul is Christ. All the promises and all the prophecies and all the laws of God, and for that matter all the institutions of God's people, are "yeah and amen" in Jesus Christ. He is the fulfillment—or through him comes the fulfillment of it all, and not apart from him. There is not, in Paul's worldview, one category of prophecies for Israel apart from Christ and another for the assembly of Christ. No, "when the time had fully come" (Gal 4:4), God's people should affirm there is one God, one Lord, one faith, one people of God involving both Jew and gentile, and one future for them all in Christ. Even the sacrificial system has been fulfilled in the once-for-all sacrifice of Christ on the cross. And if there is no need for sacrifices, then there is also no need for the Levitical priesthood or for a literal temple.

Just how radical Paul's thoroughly Old Testamental and Jewish vision of things is can be seen when we realize that the essence of ancient religion—in the ancient Near East, in the Greco-Roman world, and in Jerusalem itself before AD 70—involved priests, temples, and sacrifices. In Paul's view, the death and resurrection of Jesus changed all that, and the only sacrifice left for him to talk about is presenting ourselves as living sacrifices to God, which is defined as true or logical worship/service. Indeed, Paul was even bold enough to rewrite the Shema and say "for us there is one God, the Father, and one Lord Jesus Christ." Christ is seen as part of the divine identity to whom his converts could now pray *marana tha*—"come O Lord," knowing full well that Jews pray only to the God of the Bible.

In the end, Alan Segal was surely right: most Jews of Paul's day would have seen him as an apostate Jew, beyond the pale. Indeed, he had the marks in his body to prove that various synagogues had rejected him and his good news. Second Corinthians 11:24 sums it up well: "five times I received from the [non-Christian] Jews the forty lashes minus one." But this can mean only that as Paul traveled in the diaspora, he continued to share the good news for both Jews and gentiles in the synagogue until he was cast out. He was not recruiting gentiles to join a synagogue where Jesus's message was not honored or embraced and where the new covenant in Christ was not recognized. He might have been known as the apostle of the gentiles, which was indeed his primary focus, but he recruited both Jews and gentiles for Christ, beginning in the synagogue wherever he went.

Another anachronistic phrase applied to this whole discussion is the "parting" or "partings of the ways" between Judaism and Christianity. While there was a Jesus movement in Paul's day, there was not yet what came to be called Christianity in the second century. And Paul would have seen Jew and gentile united in the Jewish Messiah Jesus as the way forward for both Jew and gentile. This was not a parting of the ways that left Jews or Israel or the Old Testament behind, but rather a participation in THE WAY by one and all. For Paul, "in Christ" was where the fulfillment of Israel's future and Israel's mission to be a light to the nations could be found going forward.

In short, as a prophet of Paul's era once said, "this calls for wisdom," and indeed it is so complex that we are still arguing even about the proper buzzwords to discuss Paul and his controversial relationship with his fellow Jews. One thing we know from Romans 9: he was heartbroken that so many of them had rejected Jesus of Nazareth, and he had seen this played out in synagogue after synagogue during his travels. How badly he wanted them to embrace their Messiah is clear from this remark: "for I could wish myself accursed and cut off from Christ for the sake of my people, those of my own race, the people of Israel" (Rom 9:3–4). This is the same man who said "I have been crucified with Christ and I no longer live, but Christ lives in me" (Gal 2:20). There is no contradiction here, for Paul believes that God has a plan, however mysterious, for Israel and the assembly of God composed of Jew and gentile to be one people of God in the end. In the meanwhile, the good news is for Jew and gentile alike, and Galatians and Romans make that very clear indeed.

PART 2: RESPONDENTS

THINKING ABOUT SUPERSESSIONISM FROM PAUL TO MELITO OF SARDIS

LYNN H. COHICK

Rarely have I felt so uncomfortable with my Christian heritage. Rarely have its flaws been so artistically and beautifully exposed. A pound of flesh, but not a drop of blood.[1] Shakespeare's Portia (in the guise of doctor Balthazar) pronounces the verdict in favor of the Christian merchant Antonio against the Jewish moneylender Shylock. Such is the power of this phrase, "a pound of flesh," that it has become a colloquial expression for excessive debt owed to a merciless lender.[2] Even the name "Shylock" is synonymous with a loan shark who has no sympathy for his debtors. Shakespeare reflects his culture's assessment of Jewish character: greedy, lacking mercy, cruel. Negative character traits revealed themselves visually, as Jews were described as looking discontented. A contemporary of Shakespeare cited a proverb that to look like a Jew was to look

---

1. Shakespeare, *The Merchant of Venice*, Act IV, Scene 1, lines 316–17: "Shed thou no blood, nor cut thou less nor more But just a pound of flesh."

2. For a careful discussion of Jews in Shakespeare's plays, and in his London, see David Nirenberg, *Anti-Judaism: the Western Tradition* (New York: Norton, 2013), 269–99. He observes, "We are … in Shakespeare's theatrical world: a world every bit as concerned with 'Judaizing' as Luther's Germany, or the Inquisition's Spain, and every bit as willing to put that concern to work, albeit in its own way" (271).

discontented.[3] Shylock defends his decision to take his pound of flesh
with the declaration "My deeds upon my head," an allusion to the
Jewish leaders' cry against Christ, "His blood be on our heads and
upon our children's heads" (Matt 27:25).[4] As the final humiliation,
Shylock is forced to convert to Christianity.[5]

I began my essay by referencing an emotionally powerful play,
because the broad definition of Christian supersessionism carries
with it centuries of wicked deeds done in Christ's name. The fact that
the essays in this book oppose supersessionism defined as replacement, while excellent and laudable, cannot erase the past. And, of
course, these authors recognize that. Each one speaks out strongly
against anti-Semitism, including its horrific expression in the Shoah. I
want to acknowledge contemporary Jews' understandable fear when
Christians write about the place of Judaism, the role of biblical Israel,
and the supremacy of Christ. I hope my own comments on the subject,
alongside those in this book, move toward ameliorating such fears.

My understanding of the term "supersessionism" in Paul's letters
differs little from the three authors' positions stated in the preceding
essays. I concur that supersessionism understood as replacement theology is not found in Paul's letters; however, supersessionism understood as a conviction that Jesus Christ is the fulfillment of the biblical
promises of redemption for all people is consistent with Paul's gospel
message. Rather than a robust rebuttal, I offer affirming applause.

3. Nirenberg, *Anti-Judaism*, 269, citing Thomas Coryate in 1611: "'To looke like
a Jewe' ... means to look like 'one discontented.'"

4. Scripture quotations in this essay are the author's translation. Shylock's declaration comes in *Merchant of Venice*, Act IV, Scene 1, lines 195–96: "My deeds upon
my head. I crave the law, The penalty, and forfeit of my bond."

5. See *Merchant of Venice*, Act IV Scene 1, lines 379–87. Nirenberg argues,
"Shylock may bleed like a Christian, hate like a Christian, even occasionally talk like
a Christian, but he most emphatically does not become a Christian, not even after
his conversion" (Nirenberg, *Anti-Judaism*, 295). He continues, "it is not surprising
that the question of whether or not a Jew can 'turn Christian' is a crucial one in
The Merchant of Venice, with Jessica as its focus" (296). Jessica is Shylock's daughter,
who marries the Christian (gentile) Lorenzo and steals much of her father's wealth.

But merely extending agreement is hardly worth a reader's time and attention, so I hope to advance the essayists' claims further. Overall, I suggest that more attention to questions of identity in its racial, gender, and ethnic expressions, both now and in the Roman imperial period, will move the supersession conversation forward. The categories of Jew and gentile, so crucial to Paul, are only partly based on their observance (or not) of the Mosaic law. The labels are much more complex, and span cultural, salvific, and daily holiness issues. One thinks of the Judaea Capta coins minted by Vespasian to commemorate the capture of Jerusalem and destruction of the Jewish temple. The coins depict Judea as a woman bound and seated with a triumphant Roman soldier standing over her. Rome's imperial power dominated "Israel" and destroyed its temple, and the resulting displacement of Jewish identity impacted Christian (Jew and gentile) sense of self.

Additionally, I suggest the importance of the relational reality animating the Pauline refrain of being "in Christ." Being in Christ establishes relationships, on the one hand, between believers and their Lord, and, on the other, among believers within the church, Christ's body. One's identity "in Christ" does not exceed nor erase a believer's racial, gender, or ethnic distinctive. Rather, the new identity "in Christ" offers common space for those with different backgrounds, a new way to build relationships as they grow in Christ's body. Willie James Jennings emphasizes the transformational aspect of Christian identity that has been lost in our theological imagination. Christ's incarnate life was "a life of joining, belonging, connection, and intimacy."[6] I hope to weave this thread of relationship throughout my response.

I will treat each main author separately, and offer reflections or explore a trajectory from their thoughts. Additionally, I will explore a

---

6. Willie James Jennings, *The Christian Imagination: Theology and the Origins of Race* (New Haven: Yale University Press, 2010), 7. I offer my thanks to my teaching assistant, Sam Cho, for alerting me to this connection.

less-well-known second-century author, Melito of Sardis, whose *Peri Pascha* represents an early Christian expression of supersessionism. Melito points to biblical Israel to expound on the church. His sermon includes both praise for "Israel" and strong denouncement, demonstrating how, *and how not*, to think about "Israel." Finally, I explore images besides the olive tree (Rom 11) to reinforce Paul's use of metaphor to convey theological truth. In particular, both the image of the church as Christ's body and the image of the church as God's temple as presented in Ephesians[7] offer ways to imagine the relationships between the old covenant and the new covenant, between biblical Israel and first-century Jesus-followers, and between present-day Judaism and Christianity.

RESPONSE TO SCOT MCKNIGHT

McKnight points to the implicit underlying question that often drives conversations about supersessionism—namely, the evangelism of Jews by Christians. As we saw in Shakespeare's *Merchant of Venice*, Jews under Christian political rule faced the real threat of having their Judaism forcibly stripped from them in the waters of Christian baptism. Yet in Paul's environment, the power differential worked the opposite way, for the synagogue was the larger community that had (at least some of the time) political legitimacy from local authorities or from Rome.

McKnight rightly maintains that Paul's crucial point in Romans 9–11 is that gentile believers should not belittle Israel (or Jews). The metaphor of the olive tree found in Romans 11 is rightly focused upon. Another important image—the church as God's temple—further illustrates Paul's views on the relationship of Jews and gentiles in light of Christ's redemptive work. In Ephesians 2:19–22, Paul describes the church as God's temple, wherein God's Spirit dwells. Paul wrote this while the Jerusalem temple stood. This metaphor follows Paul's

---

7. On Pauline authorship of Ephesians, see Lynn H. Cohick, *Ephesians*, NICNT (Grand Rapids: Eerdmans, 2020), 61–97.

declaration that gentile believers are now members of God's family alongside God's holy people. Paul draws on Isaiah's prophetic hope that those who are far will be drawn near (Isa 57:19; Eph 2:13); Isaiah refers to Jews who are far away, while Paul substitutes gentiles who are spiritually far from the true God. Additionally, Paul asserts that Christ tore down the dividing barrier that separated gentiles from Jews, most likely drawing a figural analogy from the physical barrier separating the Jewish holy spaces in the Jerusalem temple from the court of the gentiles (2:14–15).[8] Paul's picture of believers, Jew and gentile, as stones placed side by side to create the temple's four walls highlight the superiority of being together "in Christ" as one's primary identity.

William Plevan addresses the issue of temple within Second Temple Judaism and Paul, de-centering the discussion of the Mosaic law in supersession debates. While he acknowledges that supersessionism debates today focus on whether "the commandments of the Torah are of intrinsic or merely instrumental value in fulfilling Israel's historic role,"[9] he suggests that the deeper issue revolves around the locus of holiness. He argues that perhaps the most "un-Jewish" aspect of Paul's views is his disinterest in the Jerusalem temple as the space where God's Spirit is present for both Israel and the world.[10] Plevan continues, "the most supersessionist aspect of Christian theology may not be the claim of Jesus as Messiah or as Jesus as the incarnation

---

8. Cohick, *Ephesians*, 359–60. See also Lionel J. Windsor, *Reading Ephesians and Colossians after Supersessionism* (Eugene, OR: Cascade, 2017), 133.

9. William Plevan, "Meet the New Paul, Same as the Old Paul: Michael Wychograd, Kendall Soulen, and the New Problem of Supersessionism," *Cross Currents* 59.2 (2009): 226.

10. Plevan, "Meet the New Paul," 228. Witherington observes briefly Paul's conviction about Christ's sacrifice and believers as "living sacrifices," noting the radical nature of this position, but does not follow up on this insight. Plevan critiques Soulen for failing to address the temple cult, since Soulen argues that the Hebrew Bible promotes an "economy of mutual blessing."

of God, but Jesus as a sacrifice, or the final sacrifice."[11] Plevan maintains that the rabbis concluded that God's love for Israel remains
constant beyond the temple's destruction, and that "God's holiness
works through God's election of Israel *for the sake of the world*."[12] That
is, Israel is holy because of its election, and not because of its adherence to the law.

Plevan focuses on the temple as *the* place where sinners could
offer sacrifices for their sins. Beyond forgiveness of sins is the question of holiness, which implies God's presence in some manner. With
the temple gone, the rabbis reinforced Israel's election as evidence
of God's presence among them, for the world. In the time of Paul,
however, temple holiness had another component—namely, the element of cleanliness or cultic purity that excluded certain Jews and all
gentiles from sacred spaces within the temple grounds. The issue of
purity and the corresponding gentile "impurity" permeate the pages
of the New Testament. For Paul, the ecclesial and the soteriological
are intertwined, as gentiles and Jews become one new humanity, and
one temple of God's Spirit, through Christ. Paul's insistence on gentile
cleanness and purity in Christ allows him to imagine a temple made
of gentile and Jewish "stones." From this conviction, Paul lived out
his Jewish identity, including obeying the Mosaic law to the degree
that it did not segregate him from gentile believers.

McKnight points to the second century as the period when the
church distanced itself from "the essential Israelite story" (41[13]). He
concurs with Soulen's argument against "a crude supersessionistic narrative" but invites a more nuanced "discussion about prophecy and
typology and narrative and especially the sense of fulfillment" (25).
I will take up this discussion below by examining Melito of Sardis's

---

11. Plevan, "Meet the New Paul," 228.

12. Plevan, "Meet the New Paul," 228 (italics original).

13. Page numbers in parentheses refer to the essays in Part 1 of the present
volume.

Peri Pascha, a treatise that illustrates not only Christian typology but also anti-Jewish rhetoric.

RESPONSE TO MICHAEL F. BIRD

Michael F. Bird offers a helpful summary of the various ancient Jewish groups who claimed their views and practices were superior to their fellow Jews. He argues that Paul's claim about Jesus as Messiah includes the eschatological conviction that the end of the ages has dawned with Christ's death and resurrection. Given that the present age is fading and the new day beginning, Paul maintains that gentiles *qua* gentiles could be full members of a fledgling group of Jesus followers, through faith in the Messiah Jesus. Bird concludes that Paul is no more of a supersessionist than the sectarian Jews revealed in the Dead Sea Scrolls, for Paul redefined Israel "around the Messiah and the Spirit" (46).

Bird's historical reconstruction highlights the unique position of Christianity vis-à-vis Judaism, that there is a familial relationship between them. I suggest separating the discussion of supersessionism from the general claim that devotees of any faith might claim superiority over all other forms of religion. Supersessionism is a particular claim that a sibling makes over against their brother, or a child to their parent. The term implies relationship. Distinctive qualities shared by Jews and Christians include that both faiths worship the one God as revealed in the Hebrew Bible. Both rely on the creation narrative in Genesis, and later God's calling of Abraham. Both believe that this God establishes covenants, among them the Noahic, Abrahamic, Mosaic, and Davidic. Christians hold that the covenants are fulfilled in the new covenant perfected in Christ. Pope John Paul II spoke of Judaism as "intrinsic" to Christianity, and of Jews as "our dearly beloved brothers, and, in a certain way, it could be said that you are our elder brothers."[14] After exploring this relationship further, I will address Bird's assessment of

---

14. Pope John Paul II, "The Roots of Anti-Judaism in the Christian Environment," *The New York Times*, 13 April, 1986.

Paul's argument of "interlocking destiny" in Romans by reflecting on modern conversations about Jewish identity.

Bird uses the terms "deficit" and "deficient" in describing the position of Paul's Jewish contemporaries on the topic of salvation. I am overall sympathetic to his argument, and I wish to fill out this idea by drawing on Jewish-Catholic dialogue from the Second Vatican Council, including *Nostra Aetate* (*In Our Time*) and *Lumen Gentium* (*Light of the Nations*). The latter document declared that Jews are beloved of God and called with an irrevocable calling, drawing on Romans 11:28–29.[15] Building on this foundation, Cardinal Walter Kasper develops a position that affirms the distinctive and enduring status of the Jewish covenant while also insisting on the unique status of the new, Christian covenant in Christ.[16] On the fiftieth anniversary of *Nostra Aetate*, a statement from the Commission of the Holy See for Religious Relations with the Jews incorporated Kasper's thoughts, including that Jesus's "work of salvation in the New Covenant confirms and perfects the dimensions of the Old."[17] This document, titled *The Gifts and the Calling of God Are Irrevocable (Rom 11:29)*, declares that Israel's calling stands "on the basis of God's unfailing faithfulness

---

15. *Lumen Gentium* (21 November 1964), The Holy See, https://www.vatican. va/archive/hist_councils/ii_vatican_council/documents/vat-ii_const_19641121_ lumen-gentium_en.html, paragraph 16; see also *Nostra Aetate* (28 October, 1965), The Holy See, https://www.vatican.va/archive/hist_councils/ii_vatican_council/ documents/vat-ii_decl_19651028_nostra-aetate_en.html, paragraph 4.

16. Cardinal Walter Kasper served as head of the Commission of the Holy See for Religious Relations with the Jews from 2000 to 2010. For a discussion of Kasper, see Adam Gregerman, "Superiority without Supersessionism: Walter Kasper, *The Gifts and the Calling of God Are Irrevocable*, and God's Covenant with the Jews," *Theological Studies* 79.1 (2018): 36–59.

17. *The Gifts and the Calling of God Are Irrevocable (Rom 11:29): A Reflection on Theological Questions Pertaining to Catholic-Jewish Relations on the Occasion of the 50th Anniversary of Nostra Aetate* (10 December 2015), Commission of the Holy See for Religious Relations with the Jews, http://www.vatican.va/roman_curia/pontifical_councils/chrstuni/relations-jews-docs/rc_pc_chrstuni_doc_20151210_ebraismo -nostra-aetate_en.html, paragraph 27; hereafter, this document is cited as *Gifts*.

to his people."[18] The calling begins with Abraham and is "essentially constitutive" of Christianity, because in the fullness of the promise to Abraham the universality of God's salvation is accomplished in Christ.[19] Pointing to Paul's metaphor of the olive tree in Romans 11, *Gifts* argues that God's action of grafting wild branches (gentiles) onto the trunk signals "a new dimension of God's work of salvation, so that the Christian Church cannot merely be understood as a branch or a fruit of Israel."[20] This same God made an irrevocable covenant with Israel, and, because the same God has acted, "there cannot be different paths or approaches to God's salvation."[21] And because God is at work, Israel has not "been repudiated or has lost its mission."[22]

Cardinal Kasper and *Gifts* invokes a similar attitude to that which Paul displays—namely, that these realities constitute a mystery, for "that the Jews are participants in God's salvation is theologically unquestionable, but how that can be possible without confessing Christ explicitly, is and remains an unfathomable divine mystery."[23] This response is not a *deus ex machina* but rather is based on Paul's conviction that God has hardened ethnic Israel. Bruce Longenecker rightly observes that "it is it is precisely because the Jews are God's covenant people that a part of them has experienced hardening, since God works now, as God always has worked, through both hardening and enlivenment."[24] Paul insists in Romans 9–11 that God is deeply invested in the salvation of his people, consistent with being a God who irrevocably called his people into being. Paul continues, enigmatically, that Christ is the *telos* of the law (Rom 10:4).

---

18. *Gifts*, paragraph 32

19. *Gifts*, paragraph 33.

20. *Gifts*, paragraph 33.

21. *Gifts*, paragraph 35.

22. *Gifts*, paragraph 32.

23. *Gifts*, paragraph 35.

24. Bruce Longenecker, "On Israel's God and God's Israel: Assessing Supersessionism in Paul," *JTS* 58.1 (2007) 38.

Simon Gathercole's insight is important here: he observes that this section of Romans is "unchristological"—that is, "by comparison [to chapters 1–8], in Romans 9–11 Christ *does* much less."[25] Yet when Christ displays agency, it is at a critical place in Paul's argument. Christ is the deliverer from Zion, pointing to the incarnation.[26] Christ is even now in Zion, as a stumbling stone that God uses to provoke Jews to follow Christ. The "stone" is both the solid foundation for salvation and the impediment to it. "Mercy and hardening come to clear expression at one and the same time in this 'stone,' which can be both relied upon and tripped over."[27] The presence of Christ, the mystery of "Christ in you, the hope of glory" (Col 1:27), embodies the paradox that God works out now, as hardening and invitation are simultaneously extended. J. Ross Wagner concludes similarly, "Far from being stymied by the resistance of the rest, God has commandeered their rebellion, intensifying it and channeling it to achieve God's own ends."[28] Paul explains the conviction that "all Israel will be saved" by pointing to the promised Deliverer to Zion (Isa 59:20–21). Yet Paul's confidence is based not solely on Isaiah's claim but on the gifts and calling of God, for these are irrevocable. This point is driven home by Jonathan Linebaugh, who explains, "Paul's argument does not run 'all Israel will be saved because Israel is loved on account of their ancestors,' but rather 'Israel is loved on account of their ancestors *because* (γάρ) the gifts and calling of God are

---

25. Simon Gathercole, "Locating Christ and Israel in Romans 9–11," in *God and Israel*, ed. Todd Still (Waco, TX: Baylor University Press, 2017), 115–39 (here 116).

26. Gathercole, "Locating Christ," 137.

27. Gathercole, "Locating Christ," 126. He concludes that the phrase "all Israel" (Rom 11:26) refers to "those who have been provoked by the mission to the gentiles to embrace the gospel" (136). Moreover, he argues that Christ's agency is not Paul's focus, rather "it is the *locations* of Christ in relation to Israel and the world that come to the fore in Romans 9–11" (117).

28. J. Ross Wagner, "'Enemies' Yet 'Beloved' Still: Election and the Love of God in Romans 9–11," in Still, *God and Israel*, 95–113 (here 100).

irrevocable' (11:29)."[29] Paul locates election in the Abrahamic covenant, as he argues in Romans 4. That is, the people of Israel are the
flesh and blood descendants of Jacob or have joined this group via
proselytism. Pointing to Romans 11:29 and the claim that God's calling
of Israel is irrevocable, Bird stresses that, while Jews have advantages
(Rom 3:1; 9:4–5), the relationship between Jews and gentiles should
be one of "interlocking destiny."

An alternative view is put forward by J. Brian Tucker, who connects the statement about the irrevocability of God's calling of Israel
and "a continuing role for Torah as a demarcator of the Jewish people
and their identity."[30] Tucker's claims raise the interesting point as to
where election might be grounded: Is it in ethnic or cultural heritage
or in the practice of the Torah? Rabbi Donniel Hartman discusses
the current difficulty in developing a shared definition of "Jew" that
includes community life. "I understood that if Jewish collective life
was to be possible, by which I mean a Jewish peoplehood that can
transcend denominational lines and include all factions of Jewish
life, we need to develop an approach to boundaries that allow for a
common ground in which all can participate despite our differences."[31]
Hartman recognizes that some Jews today express their identity as
atheists and nonobservant.[32] Thus a definition of "Jew" and "Judaism"

---

29. Jonathan A. Linebaugh, "Not the End: The History and Hope of the Unfailing
Word in Romans 9–11," in Still, *God and Israel*, 141–63 (here 157).

30. J. Brian Tucker, *Reading Romans After Supersessionism: The Continuation of
Jewish Covenantal Identity* (Eugene, OR: Cascade, 2018), 9.

31. Donniel Hartman, *The Boundaries of Judaism* (London: Continuum, 2007),
10. He argues for a boundary that celebrates diversity and holds to a "presumption
of loyalty, by which I mean an *a priori* decision to work to ensure that one's boundary policies encompass as wide a spectrum of those who identity (*sic*) themselves
as Jews as possible" (169).

32. I suggest that the election of Israel, rooted in the Abrahamic covenant,
includes but is not limited by the Mosaic covenant. I am not sure how much of a
parallel we might claim between modern Jewry's wide diversity and the first-century
world, with its diaspora Jews and the Judean sectarian expressions. For example, few
if any Jews in the ancient world would have been atheists (and few gentiles for that

for many Jews is not (only) a description of religious conviction but a cultural expression. Additionally, some practices have religious overtones for some Jews and only cultural meaning for others (e.g., lighting Shabbat candles). Tucker's insistence, then, on Torah-observance as the identifier of Jews and Judaism would not align fully with contemporary Jewish thought on Jewish peoplehood.

RESPONSE TO BEN WITHERINGTON III

Ben Witherington III examines Paul's argument about Christ and the Mosaic law in Galatians. Drawing on Galatians, Witherington takes up arguments from the Paul-within-Judaism movement. This position explores Paul's Jewish identity, and Witherington focuses on the relative value of Jewish religious life vis-à-vis the believer's identity in Christ. Witherington draws on John Barclay's argument that God's creative act in Christ, his gift to Jew and Greek alike, overcomes cosmic Sin and Death.[33] Witherington explains that Paul's claim that through the law "I died" to the law (Gal 2:19) is more subtle that a "simple binary choice between comprehensive obedience to the law and utter repudiation of it" (70). He agrees with Barclay that there was a rather wide variety of praxis among Jews in Paul's time. Witherington concludes with Alan Segal that most first-century Jews would have considered Paul an apostate Jew (78).[34]

This assessment raises questions about how diaspora Jews negotiated their lives in urban, pagan cities. Paul indicates that his message, given repeatedly in synagogues, was ultimately judged unacceptable by a majority of Jews, and he was given the lash (2 Cor 11:24). What

---

matter). Jews in the Greco-Roman world were known by three practices: circumcision, Sabbath rest, and a refusal to eat pork.

33. John M. G. Barclay, *Jews in the Mediterranean Diaspora: From Alexander to Trajan (323 BCE–117 CE)* (Edinburgh: T&T Clark, 1996). See also John M. G. Barclay, the "An Identity Received from God: The Theological Configuration of Paul's Kinship Discourse," *Early Christianity* 8 (2017): 354–72.

34. Alan F. Segal, *Paul the Convert: The Apostolate and Apostasy of Saul the Pharisee* (New Haven: Yale University Press, 1990).

precisely was unacceptable might be discerned from Paul's account of Peter's time in Antioch, described in Galatians 2. Witherington rightly notes the two-fold issue. Paul does not want gentile believers circumcised,[35] and he expects believers, Jews and gentiles, to share table fellowship. Underneath the presenting problem of table fellowship is the concern that gentiles are unclean and their food is unclean. Witherington cites compelling evidence that Jews maintained food laws, especially refusing pork, unto death.

Yet Paula Fredriksen cautions that the situation with diaspora Jews might be more nuanced.[36] While Fredriksen and Witherington agree that the source of friction was table fellowship, Witherington disputes Fredriksen's reconstruction of diaspora Jewish life as one highly integrated into urban realities, such that Jews would have entered the homes of their pagan friends and drunk wine served by pagans.[37] Fredriksen, rightly in my estimation, reminds readers that wine prepared in an unkosher manner might have raised sensibilities of those who traveled to Antioch or to the West from Judea or Galilee, but it might not have been such a problem for those who would not have reasonable access to wine prepared in Galilee. Fredriksen correctly points out that gentile believers' homes might have pagan idols still present, especially if only the wife was a believer. Jews from the Jewish homeland might express a hesitancy to enter such an abode (see Acts 10:25–29), but diaspora Jews had practice in negotiating such realities. Finally, Fredriksen points to gentile *qua* gentile attendance in synagogues and the outer court of the Jerusalem Temple, concluding that their presence tells us little about the law observance of faithful Jews.

---

35. And presumably Paul resists any demands on female gentile believers to identify as Jews, perhaps by circumcising their sons.

36. Paula Fredriksen, *Paul: The Pagans' Apostle* (New Haven: Yale University Press, 2017), 97.

37. Fredriksen, *Paul: The Pagans' Apostle*, 98: "In the view of James's men, consuming food and wine (which may have been offered to idols) *within a pagan household that itself would hold images of gods* was a further concession to gentile participation than they were prepared to make" (italics original).

Witherington speaks of the Mosaic law having "an important function in its day and time, [but] its day and time had come and gone," and also declares that Paul does not "see Christianity as replacing Judaism" (74). The assessment that the function of the law has come and gone captures Paul's agitated mood in Galatians but downplays his more nuanced evaluation of the law. Witherington speaks of the believers' new identity in Christ as in some way transcending and relativizing ethnic identities (68). I suggest that we might want to distinguish between the categories of "ethnic identity" and "the praxis that goes with it," as the latter was much debated among Jews in Paul's day (and continues today) while the ethnic identification as a Jew was a given. Conflating "law observance" and "Jew" mutes the crucial note of election of Israel by God, through Abraham and Sarah. Shaye Cohen explains that ancient Jewish identity centered on (a) religious, cultural, and political affiliation and (b) ethnicity and geography.[38] The latter was a matter of birth, the former of choice. Ethnic identity, being a Jew (or Judean), was a permanent reality from birth; in contrast, Paul's Roman citizenship, while also attained at birth, could be stripped if he committed certain crimes. Paul's religious affiliation was first that of Pharisee and then as apostle of Christ to the gentiles. The rhetoric in Acts against Stephen and Paul suggests that Jewish leaders considered these men to be Jews who spoke or acted falsely and should be punished based on Jewish laws (Acts 6:11–7:58; 23:5–10). Said another way, some Jews may have considered Paul a (very) bad Jew, but a Jew nonetheless.

Witherington demonstrates this model in his interpretation of Galatians 6:16 (77). He argues that the phrase "Israel of God" refers to ethnic, non-believing Jews. Paul asks a blessing of peace and mercy on his community and on his fellow Jews. Adam Gregerman, a Jewish scholar who works in the field of Jewish-Catholic dialogue, argues that the Catholic church has moved from a replacement supersessionism to a non-supersessionary position that maintains a "vital continuity"

---

38. Shaye J. D. Cohen, *The Beginnings of Jewishness: Boundaries, Varieties, Uncertainties* (Berkeley: University of California Press, 1999), 70–92.

between the promises of the old covenant and the fulfillment of God's plan in Christ and his new covenant.[39] Gregerman concludes that by drawing on a good/better paradigm, the Jews' "lesser covenant is not worthless or invalid. On the contrary, it is good, for it is from God and has value, even after Christ."[40]

From a different vantage point, Jennings emphasizes the importance of maintaining the particularity of Israel, as the failure to do so has resulted in European Christianity elevating the ideal of universalism and then defining it as equivalent to white European culture. Jennings reminds us that Jesus was present in space and time, allowing us to see God at work in the world, and "that seeing comes with Christian bodies, their participation in the divine work in the world, drawing them towards other peoples, calling them to become one and to love concretely."[41] Jennings argues that when Jew-and-gentile identities disappeared within the Christian imagination, Christian hubris with its "white supremacist imaginings" took hold.[42] "Rather than the possibility of new identity rooted in the resurrected Son of God, an identity that draws definition from our cultural realities yet is determined by a new reality of love and belonging, colonialist new identity meant unrelenting assimilation and the enfolding of lives and cultural practices inside processes of commodification."[43]

MELITO OF SARDIS AND HIS *PERI PASCHA*

As McKnight observes, the insistence on fulfillment as the best lens through which to see the relationship between Judaism and Christianity is not a new idea. It resonates in certain ways with a second-century work, *Peri Pascha*, by Melito of Sardis. Specifically, Melito's hermeneutical method stresses comparison of the sketch

---

39. Gregerman, "Superiority without Supersessionism," 48.

40. Gregerman, "Superiority without Supersessionism," 56.

41. Jennings, *Christian Imagination*, 167.

42. Jennings, *Christian Imagination*, 292.

43. Jennings, *Christian Imagination*, 292.

and the final work, the model and the completed reality.[44] He argues
that while the sketch is not the final product, neither does the reality
occur *ex nihilo*. Second-century Christian authors searched for the
literal (historical) and figural (deeper, perhaps hidden) meanings in
a text. Often the latter was gained through typology. Interpreters of
Scripture looked for referents, the reality to which language pointed,
for "language was symbolic, and its meaning lay in that to which it
referred."[45] For Melito, the referent that unlocked the mystery was
Christ. There is one mystery, because there is one Christ, and this
single mystery is discovered in both old and new.

In the *Peri Pascha*, Melito employs typology to Old Testament
events and people to discover models for Christ. In the New Testament,
Paul uses τύπος (type, pattern), for example, when speaking of Adam
as a type of Christ (Rom 5:14). In the *Peri Pascha*, we read that "what
once was precious (τίμιον) becomes worthless (ἄτιμον) when what
is truly precious has been revealed" (PP 37), and "the model (τύπος)
then was precious before the reality (ἀληθείας), and the parable was
marvelous before the interpretation; that is, the people (ὁ λαὸς) was
precious before the church (ἐκκλησίαν) arose, and the law (ὁ νόμος)
was marvelous before the gospel was elucidated" (PP 41).[46]

Typology includes a mimetic function, which Paul emphasizes
when encouraging the Philippians to model his behavior (Phil 3:17).
Melito makes full use of this aspect of "type" as he draws on moral
examples from the Old Testament narrative to explain and support
Christian life and liturgy. Later, both Origen (*Cels.* 3.3) and Irenaeus
(*Haer.* 4.3.1) cite ancient Israel and Jewish history as holding examples

44. For a general discussion, see Lynn H. Cohick, "Intertextuality in Melito
of Sardis," in *Intertextuality in the Second Century*, ed. Jeffrey Bingham and Clayton
Jefford (Leiden: Brill, 2016), 126–49.

45. Frances M. Young, *Biblical Exegesis and the Formation of Christian Culture*
(Peabody, MA: Hendrickson, 2002), 120.

46. S. G. Hall, *Melito of Sardis on Pascha and Fragments* (Oxford: Clarendon
Press, 1979), 18–21.

for godly behavior.[47] Regarding the biblical text, Melito's attention is primarily at the narrative level, rather than spotlighting specific words. He explores the Passover story from Exodus and creates a larger narrative that explains human suffering and death's defeat by Christ, through his passion.

The homily's structure includes two halves of roughly equal length, separated by a middle section that exposes the plight of humanity under sin's power. In the first half, the Old Testament narrative offers numerous positive examples that illuminate Christ and godly virtues. In the center of the homily, Melito weaves together the Old Testament narrative of the human fall and the redemption of Israel from Egypt with the passion and deliverance of humanity in Christ. The second half of the homily demonstrates how "Jesus fulfills the prophets' promises, [and] Jesus' salvific qualities are underscored, often in direct opposition to Israel's alleged responsibility for the passion."[48]

Interestingly, the homily never uses the terms "Jew" or "Judaism." Instead, we find the people ($\delta\ \lambda\alpha\delta\varsigma$) used eighteen times, often carrying a positive connotation, while "Israel" is blamed for the crucifixion (PP 73, 74, 76, 77, 81, 87, 96). "The people" typically refers to (a) the ancient Israelites in the Passover story (Exod 12), (b) those who offer a type that is now fulfilled by the church, or (c) those who did not lament at Christ's crucifixion (PP 98). I argue that Melito does not intend to speak about Jewish contemporaries, but rather focuses on Old Testament and New Testament biblical characters.[49] He builds a

---

47. Interestingly, Theophilus of Antioch, writing around 180 CE, does not engage the question of Jews or Judaism. See Lynn H. Cohick, *The Peri Pascha Attributed to Melito of Sardis: Setting, Purpose, and Sources*, Brown Judaic Studies 327 (Providence: Brown University, 2000), 87: "Within the same city (though with about 150 years between them) Theophilus and Chrysostom express different attitudes about Jews and/or Judaism."

48. Cohick, Peri Pascha *Attributed to Melito*, 3.

49. Cohick, Peri Pascha *Attributed to Melito*, 54–56. Nirenberg makes the same observation—that trying to explain Christian anxieties about Judaism based on "'real Jews' ignores the ability of Christian thought to generate Judaism 'out of its own

rhetorical "Jew" that serves as a foil for his construction of Christian identity. This pattern continued in the church—for example, informing Shakespeare's Shylock and the Christians in Venice.

Melito claims the etymology of "Israel" is to "see God" (PP 82) and then asserts that "Israel" was never a model for the church, as it never saw God.[50] The "Israel" of the homily's second half models the Egyptians' rejection of God and their subsequent suffering of the plagues discussed in the homily's earlier passages. "Israel" is contrasted with Jesus and is responsible for his death. Melito has the unhappy honor of being the earliest known Christian author to declare that "God" has been murdered, "the King of Israel" has been killed by an "Israelite right hand" (PP 96). In sum, "the characteristics of 'Israel' in the homily's anti-Jewish section seem to define the group as those Jews who participated in the passion, as presented in canonical and noncanonical gospel accounts."[51] In this, the Peri Pascha differs from later texts, such as Chrysostom's work that highlights specific interactions between Christians and Jews in fourth-century Antioch.[52] While I maintain that Melito describes Jews contemporary with Jesus, it is possible that his listeners took a further step to implicate their Jewish neighbors. We know that when the church gained political power, it did precisely that.

Additionally, the categories of old and new, type and reality, pertain to Christian self-definition, as seen in the active battle between the emerging orthodox group and followers of Marcion. Melito's community may have been threatened by Marcionism. To combat claims that the God of the Old Testament was inconsistent or worse,

---

entrails'" (Anti-Judaism, 272). I disagree with Nirenberg's follow-up comment that Paul believed that "the threat of 'Judaizing' attends every Christian act of communication, interaction, and exchange."

50.   Cohick (Peri Pascha Attributed to Melito, 55) notes that "Israel" and ὁ λαός are used interchangeably in PP 16, 30, 31.

51.   Cohick, Peri Pascha Attributed to Melito, 57.

52.   Chrysostom, Hom. in Rom. 12.20.3 on Sabbath; Disc. 1.2–5 on festivals and oath taking.

second-century Christians explained that the Mosaic law was a necessity because Jews were inferior, stubborn, or ignorant of God's grace.[53]
In this intra-Christian argument, the emerging *regula fidei* position
used the category of "symbolic Jews" as a foil to promote Christian
theology or practices. Therefore, the *Peri Pascha*'s use of "old" and
"new" could be "an attempt to wrestle out of Marcion's hand the definition of Christianity as a 'new' faith."[54]

> This is essentially an intra-Christian problem, one springing
> from Christianity's developing theology/Christology, not from
> interaction with Jews directly. Questions about whether and
> how to follow the Law (or why Christians do not follow the
> Law, but claim the books of the Law as their own), or about
> why Jews have not (yet?) followed Jesus the Messiah need not
> come from Jews, but can be and were raised by Christians and
> pagan critics alike.[55]

Melito's *Peri Pascha* is an example of a second-century author
reading a key Old Testament story, the Passover, through the lens
of both Genesis 3 (the fall of humanity) and Jesus's passion. The
homily stresses fulfillment of the type. In this, we see similarities to
Paul's claims about Christ as fulfillment. The homily condemns New
Testament Jewish characters who failed to see Christ as Messiah, using
typology to link the Jews of Jesus's day with the biblical archenemy
of Israel, the Egyptians. In this, Melito diverges sharply from Paul's

---

53. David Efroymson, "The Patristic Connection," in *Anti-Semitism and the
Foundations of Christianity*, ed. Alan T. Davies (New York: Paulist, 1979), 101, speaks
of the "anti-Judaic myth" used by patristic authors to defend their form of Christianity
against other Christian groups, and over against pagan views. This myth assumes
the inferiority of aspects of the Old Testament, and seeks to protect the OT God by
blaming the inferiority on the people of God.

54. Cohick, Peri Pascha *Attributed to Melito*, 84.

55. Cohick, Peri Pascha *Attributed to Melito*, 82. If this perspective is correct,
then we should not draw historical conclusions about the social relationship between
Jews and Christians from this homily.

assessment that Israel has stumbled but not fallen, that some branches have been broken off but can be regrafted onto the olive tree, the people of God.

CONCLUSION

Shakespeare's Shylock the Jew represents the fearful "other" over against which Christians in his day defined themselves. His Othello, a Moor, functioned in a similar manner, signaling the inferiority of dark skin. Jennings observes that the theological distortion evident in European colonialism, "was the replacement of Israel, or, in its proper theological term, supersessionism ... [wherein] the church replaces Israel in the mind and heart of God."[56] Jennings argues that Europeans reimagined Israel's election, replacing the visual markers of its election with a racial marker, the white body. Jennings explains that, in this view, "salvation in black bodies is doubtful, as it was in (Christian) Jews and Moors."[57] Jennings's astute and heartbreaking analysis exposes the tragic failure to listen to and be transformed by the gospel message. Paul reinterpreted the Mosaic covenant such that it no longer functioned to divide Jewish and gentile believers in Christ. Said another way, gentiles need not become proselytes to enjoy full fellowship with Jewish believers; together, the two have become one new humanity (Eph 2:14–15). The conversation about supersessionism today should take account of new studies about identity and embodiment as they relate to forming relationships between individuals and groups. The questions about obeying the law in Paul can be framed by stressing identity in Christ, and within this identity celebrating the distinct tribe, language, tongue, and nation of each believer.

---

56. Jennings, *Christian Imagination*, 32; my thanks to my teaching assistant, Sam Cho, for alerting me to this connection.

57. Jennings, *Christian Imagination*, 35.

A MESSIANIC JEWISH
RESPONSE

DAVID J. RUDOLPH

I ask, then, has God rejected his people? By no
means! ... As regards election, they are beloved for
the sake of their forefathers. For the gifts and the calling of God are irrevocable.[1]

—*Romans 11:1, 28–29*

In 2019 I had the pleasure of attending a public debate between
N. T. Wright and Mark Kinzer, a Messianic Jew, that focused on
two questions: (1) Are non-Messianic Jews members of God's
covenanted people? And (2) if so, do they as a people have a unique
covenantal calling that distinguishes their calling from that of every
other society or nation?[2] Sitting among the audience of eight hundred
people at Samford University, I looked forward to hearing Wright's
response. He is known for his depth of insight and clarity. However,
in my experience, he is often silent when it comes to the election of
the Jewish people after the coming of the Messiah. The debate at

---

1. Unless otherwise indicated, Scripture quotations are from the English Standard
Version.

2. Samford University, "A Debate on the Meaning of Israel featuring N. T. Wright
and Mark Kinzer," Provost Distinguished Lecture Series bulletin, 11 September 2019,
2. Samford's recording of the debate is available on YouTube.

Samford provided an opportunity for Wright to clarify his views on this matter and set the record straight about whether he believes the Jewish people remain God's chosen people today.

In his opening comments, Kinzer underscored God's fidelity to Israel: "God remains faithful to the genealogical descendants of Abraham, Isaac, and Jacob even when Israel is unfaithful. And this eternal fidelity grounds the church's assurance that she and the world will not be abandoned despite their own infidelity."[3] In support of this view, Kinzer pointed to Romans 11:16: "If the part of the dough offered as firstfruits is holy [Messianic Jews], then the whole batch is holy [the Jewish people]; if the root [Messiah and/or the patriarchs] is holy, then the branches are holy [all Israel]."[4] For Kinzer, Jewish people who do not believe in Jesus continue to be members of God's people, and they retain a unique covenantal calling that sets them apart from the nations.

Wright's opening statement was eloquent, and he cited more than a dozen biblical texts related to the meaning of Israel.[5] When it came to the two questions, however, his words became markedly ambiguous. To the first question, Wright said that Jewish people who do not believe in Jesus are beloved for the sake of the fathers and that Paul argues "against the idea that the Jews who do not currently believe are automatically excluded. Rather, they remain among those who in some sense or other are to be explored." I wasn't sure what that meant. To the second question, he said:

> I don't see that [covenantal] calling as such in Scripture. I see a possibility, and with that possibility I see something whose analog, I think, is sacred space [such as the Western Wall in Jerusalem]. ... As with sacred space, so with chosen people. There is a memory, there is a holiness, there is something

---

3. Quotations are from the recording of the debate (see note 2).

4. Kinzer's translation. He also referenced Luke 13:34–35; Acts 1:6; 3:19–21; Rom 9:4–6; 11:11–12, 15, 28.

5. Gen 15; 2 Sam 7; Ps 2; 87; Isa 11; 49; Rom 2:25–29; 4:16; 8–10; 11:23; 15; 1 Cor 7; Gal 3, 4; Phil 3; Heb 11–12; Rev 21.

which as Christians we respect and which we honor and we long to see coming to whatever fulfillment God has.

Again, I wasn't clear on what he meant exactly. However, the implications of his prevaricating seemed to be that the Jewish people no longer remained in covenant relationship with God.[6] Wright's "sacred space" perspective on the Jewish people reminded me of Augustine's view of Jewish customs in the apostolic period:

> For now, after the coming of the faith which had been prefigured in those observances and revealed after the death and resurrection of the Lord, these rituals had lost, as it were, their vital role. They had to be treated rather like the bodies of dead relatives which must be carried out for burial not as a matter of form but with true reverence.[7]

The Wright-Kinzer debate came to mind as I read the essays in this volume. Like Wright's equivocating, Scot McKnight, Mike Bird, and Ben Witherington do not clearly state whether they believe the Jewish people continue to be in a unique covenant relationship with God. It seems to me there is a lot of beating around the bush in the essays when it comes to this issue. Occasional statements are made that refer to God's faithfulness to the Jewish people, but such comments are often in passing, few and far between, and typically preceded by descriptions of the church as the "Israel of God" or the "one people of God." Also, there is a difference between saying that God remains faithful to the Jewish people (which could refer to Messianic Jews only) and saying that God continues to be in a covenant relationship with the Jewish people whether or not they are believers in

---

6. Gerald McDermott, Anglican Chair of Divinity at Beeson Divinity School, who moderated the event, arrived at the same conclusion: "Sadly ... [Wright] revealed that he does not believe that covenant is ongoing" (Deborah Pardo-Kaplan, "N. T. Wright and Mark Kinzer Meet at Samford University," *Kesher: A Journal of Messianic Judaism* 37 (2020): 4.

7. Augustine, *Ep.* 82.

the Messiah. Similarly, saying that Jewish people can be saved or that God has a future plan for the Jewish people is not the same as saying there remains a unique covenant relationship.

I hope the present book's "Concluding Reflections" will address this matter by answering the two questions raised in the Wright-Kinzer debate: (1) Are non-Messianic Jews members of God's covenanted people? And (2) if so, do they as a people have a unique covenantal calling that distinguishes their calling from that of every other society or nation? If the authors of Part 1 cannot affirm either, it would be helpful to understand why they think God withdrew his election of the Jewish people. It is important to hear their perspective on these questions, so the reader can understand the kind of theology being advocated and its ethical implications in relation to the Jewish people as a whole.

Another reason I mention the Wright-Kinzer debate is that the first two authors of this volume lift up Wright as a trailblazer of the kind of theology they are promoting when it comes to a Christian view of Israel, and their cases build on Wright's four decades of work in this area. For this reason, I think it is important to take a closer look at Wright's theology of Israel and understand what is at stake in following this direction and how it impacts the local church's view of the Jewish people and Jewish life.

WRIGHT'S "REDEFINED ISRAEL"

In Wright's ecclesial vision, the unique calling, responsibilities, and privileges of the Jewish people have been expropriated by God and given to the church (the redefined Israel) through the Messiah's death and resurrection. Wright's earliest formulation of this transference theology can be found in his 1980 Oxford thesis:

> In Rom. 5–8 Paul develops the picture of the church in terms belonging to Israel. This *transfer* is achieved in two stages. First, Israel's calling, responsibilities and privileges have been taken over by the Messiah himself, alone: second, what is true of the

Messiah is reckoned to be true of his people. ... In him all believers, without distinction of race, *inherit all that was Israel's.* ...
Paul, in line with Old Testament prophecy, claims that God's
glory has been *taken away from Israel according to the flesh and
given to the community of the new covenant.* ... *The Christian is
the true Jew.* ... The first five verses of the chapter [Rom 5:1–5]
thus set out the grounds of assurance in terms of the *transfer* of
Israel's privileges to the church. ... What Israel should have done,
the Messiah has done alone. Having therefore taken Israel's task,
he (and hence his people) *inherit Israel's privileges.* ... We have
seen that Paul explicitly and consciously *transfers* blessings from
Israel according to the flesh to the Messiah, and thence to the
church. ... In the same way, Gal. 2–4 argues precisely that the
worldwide believing church is the true family of Abraham, and
that those who remain as "Israel according to the flesh" are in
fact the theological descendants of Hagar and Ishmael, *with
no title to the promises.* ... It is not therefore without a touch of
bitter irony, reminiscent of Phil. 3.2ff., that he [Paul] *transfers*
the name "Israel" to the church.[8]

Wright has consistently maintained this "transfer of privilege" perspective in his writings. For example, in *The Climax of the Covenant,*
he writes that God "has systematically *transferred* the privileges and
attributes of 'Israel' to the Messiah and his people. It is therefore
greatly preferable to take 'all Israel' in v. 26 [of Rom 11] as a typically
Pauline polemical redefinition, as in Galatians 6.16 ... and in line
also with Philippians 3.2ff., where the church is described as 'the circumcision.'"[9] Wright often emphasizes the positive side of transfer
(i.e., what the church has received according to his paradigm) while

---

8. N. T. Wright, "The Messiah and the People of God: A Study in Pauline
Theology with Particular Reference to the Argument of the Epistle to the Romans"
(DPhil thesis, University of Oxford, 1980), 135–37, 139–40, 193, 196 (italics mine).

9. N. T. Wright, *The Climax of the Covenant: Christ and the Law in Pauline Theology*
(Minneapolis: Fortress, 1993), 250 (italics mine).

deemphasizing or remaining silent about the flip side (what Jews have lost).

It is beyond the scope of this response to offer a detailed critique of Wright's transference theology. Joel Kaminsky and Mark Reasoner, among others, have done an excellent job of this.[10] Having read both sides, I am convinced that when the smoke and mirrors are removed, Wright's "redefined Israel" view is ultimately a form of traditional supersessionism that is in continuity with the tradition of Justin Martyr's transference theology.[11] At the end of the day, Wright seems to maintain that the election and covenantal particularity of the Jewish people expired after the coming of the Messiah, the very error that Paul warned his gentile readers to avoid in Romans 11.

In the following two sections, I will take up the question of how Wright's expiration theology impacts a Christian view of Jews and Jewish life, particularly within the local church.

---

10. Joel Kaminsky and Mark Reasoner, "The Meaning and Telos of Israel's Election: An Interfaith Response to N. T. Wright's Reading of Paul," *Harvard Theological Review* 112:4 (2019): 421–46; Michael F. Bird, "N. T. Wright and Paul's Supersessionism: A Response to Kaminsky and Reasoner," *Harvard Theological Review* 113:4 (2020): 498–512; Joel Kaminsky and Mark Reasoner, "In Quest of a Coherent Portrait of Paul: A Rejoinder to Michael Bird," *Harvard Theological Review* 113:4 (2020): 513–27; Gregory Tatum, "Law and Covenant in *Paul and the Faithfulness of God*," in *God and the Faithfulness of Paul: A Critical Examination of the Pauline Theology of N. T. Wright*, ed. Christoph Heilig, J. Thomas Hewitt and Michael F. Bird (Tübingen: Mohr Siebeck, 2016), 318–19; Paula Fredriksen, review of *Paul and the Faithfulness of God*, by N. T. Wright, *Catholic Biblical Quarterly* 77 (2015): 387–91; Larry Hurtado, review of *Paul and the Faithfulness of God*, by N. T. Wright, *Theology* 117 (2014): 361–65; Michael G. Vanlaningham, "An Evaluation of N. T. Wright's View of Israel in Romans 11," *Bibliotheca Sacra* 170 (2013): 179–93; A. Andrew Das, *Solving the Romans Debate* (Minneapolis: Fortress, 2007), 236–45; Simon Chan, *Liturgical Theology: The Church as Worshiping Community* (Downers Grove: InterVarsity, 2006), 24–27; Douglas Harink, *Paul among the Postliberals: Pauline Theology beyond Christendom and Modernity* (Grand Rapids: Brazos, 2003), 151–84.

11. "And hence you [Trypho] ought to understand that [the gifts] formerly among your nation have been transferred to us" (Justin, *Dial.* 82).

A PERNICIOUS KIND
OF SUPERSESSIONISM

Some kinds of supersessionism are benign[12] and others contain within their DNA a kind of cancer cell that harms the body of Messiah. I would say that Wright's brand of supersessionism is the more pernicious kind, because it leads to the erasure of Jewish identity and thereby calls into question the character of the God of Jesus the Messiah. Since the body of Messiah, according to Paul, is made up of Jews and gentiles (Eph 2:15),[13] any attempt to erase the Jewish part of the body is a serious offense against a covenant partner and a major concern of Messianic Jewish leaders.[14] Joel Willitts identifies this mutation in Wright's theology and describes it as Wright's (unintentional) tendency toward fostering the erasure of Jews within the church:

> But still prevalent today, and perhaps more insidious because of its unconsciousness, is the *unintentional* interpretation of the NT that over time *fosters* the erasure *again* of Jewish ethnic presence within the church. These readings, while able to dodge accusations of overt supersessionism with great bluster (I have in mind N. T. Wright's recent work on Paul), effect the exact same outcome as their more overt sibling.[15]

---

12. E.g., McKnight suggests that "claiming religious truth" is a kind of supersessionism (page 16 of the present volume).

13. The body of Messiah represents "one new man out of two" (NET), not "one new man in place of the two" (ESV). See Lionel J. Windsor, *Reading Ephesians & Colossians after Supersessionism: Christ's Mission through Israel to the Nations* (Eugene: Cascade, 2017), 143–46.

14. Stuart Dauermann, *Converging Destinies: Jews, Christians, and the Mission of God* (Eugene: Cascade, 2017), 37–44, 48; Pardo-Kaplan, "N. T. Wright and Mark Kinzer," 7–8.

15. Joel Willitts, "Jewish Fish (ΙΧΘΥΣ) in Post-supersessionist Water: Messianic Judaism within a Post-supersessionistic Paradigm," *HTS Teologiese Studies/Theological Studies* 72.4 (2016): 3.

Wright's variety of supersessionism also has negative implications for Jews outside the church. It naturally leads to the view among Christians that Jews are no longer needed in the world and ideally should be phased out. Orthodox Jewish theologian Michael Wyschogrod explains this dynamic that has repeated itself throughout history:

> In the past ... Jews who became Catholics were supposed to act like all other Catholics. The fact that they had once been Jews had no current significance. The Church was guided by the words of Paul (Gal. 3:28): "There is neither Jew nor Greek, there is neither slave nor free, there is neither male nor female: for you are all one in Christ Jesus." In Christ, all distinctions fall away and the obligations of Christians who had been Jews are no different than the obligations of Christians who had been gentiles. In fact, throughout the centuries, Jews who entered the Church very quickly lost their Jewish identity. Within several generations they intermarried and the Jewish traces disappeared. The only exceptions to this rule were Jewish converts in Spain and Portugal, the sincerity of whose conversions was questioned and who retained a Catholic identity tinged with some Jewish elements. But this was never sanctioned by the Church. In short, if all Jews in past ages had followed the advice of the Church to become Christians, there would be no more Jews in the world today. The question we must ask is: *Does the Church really want a world without Jews? Does the Church believe that such a world is in accordance with the will of God? Or does the Church believe that it is God's will, even after the coming of Jesus, that there be a Jewish people in the world? As I have already said, the answer of the old theology to this question was clear. The Church was the new Israel and there was no further need for the old Israel. If the old Israel insisted on surviving, it was only because it did not recognize its redeemer and continued to wait for him who had already appeared. Were all Jews to*

*recognize the truth, they would cease their stubborn insistence on continuing to exist as an identifiable people and become an integral part of the new Israel—the Church—*which is God's new covenant partner in the world. The disappearance of the Jews from the world would be no theological loss because their place would have been taken by the new people of God.[16]

From a Jewish-Christian relations perspective, Wright's decision to openly embrace a form of supersessionism that views most Jews as former members of the people of God, and to promote this widely within the church in popular and academic settings, sets a dangerous precedent. Kendall Soulen puts it this way:

Christians have attempted to address the problem of economic supersessionism in a variety of ways. One possibility is simply to embrace it more or less openly as a necessary feature of Christian faith, as N. T. Wright has espoused. ... A difficulty with this option is that it seems too continuous with historic patterns of thought whose catastrophic consequences occasioned the church's self-examination with respect to the Jews in the first place. As Franklin Littell warned, "To teach that a people's mission in God's providence is finished, that they have been relegated to the limbo of history, has murderous implications, which murders will in time spell out."[17]

Since McKnight lifts up Wright as "the most significant New Testament scholar in the world today" (26[18]), I think it is important

---

16. Michael Wyschogrod, "A Letter to Cardinal Lustiger," in *Abraham's Promise: Judaism and Jewish-Christian Relations*, ed. R. Kendall Soulen (Grand Rapids: Eerdmans, 2004), 207–08 (italics mine).

17. R. Kendall Soulen, "Supersessionism," in *Encyclopedia of Jewish-Christian Relations Online*, ed. Walter Homolka et al. (Berlin: De Gruyter, 2020). Soulen cites N. T. Wright, *Paul and the Faithfulness of God* (Minneapolis: Fortress, 2013), 810; Franklin Littell, *The Crucifixion of the Jews* (New York: Harper & Row, 1975) 2.

18. Page numbers in parentheses refer to the essays in Part 1 of the present volume.

to understand exactly how his brand of supersessionism fosters the erasure of Jews in the local church.

A THEOLOGY OF JEWISH ERASURE

Wright claims that the church is composed of Jews and gentiles in Messiah. However, his ultimate vision of the church is that it is a *tertium genus* (third race). Wright explains:

> Qumran itself held an embryonic 'third entity' view of itself, marked out against the wicked world of paganism but also, necessarily, against the majority of Jews. I submit, therefore, that though Paul himself does not use the phrase 'third race', and though we have to be careful to anchor 'race' to its ancient rather than its modern use and connotations, something like that idea is not only Pauline but retains a quintessential, if characteristically paradoxical, Jewish character and flavour.[19]

The classic idea of a third race is that Christians leave behind their respective Jewish/gentile identities and become part of a new corporate entity. In Wright's model, the third entity is the Israel of

---

19. Wright, *Paul and the Faithfulness of God*, 1448. Wright describes his theology of Israel as "sectarian supersessionism," similar to Qumran's (Wright, *Paul and the Faithfulness of God*, 809). However, a major difference between Wright's view and the DSS community is that Wright's supersessionism leads to the deterritorialization of Jewish identity and the erasure of Jews. As Tucker notes, "Wright's fulfillment reworking leaves nothing of Israel's covenantal identity in its wake. ... Wright's claim in regards to Qumran also omits attention to the restoration in the land. For Qumran, restoration to the land is still expected once the temple has been cleansed. Thus, the land promise is only in a holding pattern. For Wright, the promise for restoration in the land has been swept away with the arrival of Jesus. While Wright thinks his approach does not amount to supersessionism since it is similar to Qumran's, it is not actually as similar as he maintains" (J. Brian Tucker, *Reading Romans after Supersessionism: The Continuation of Jewish Covenantal Identity* [Eugene: Cascade, 2018], 135n90).

God, in which everyone becomes a spiritual Jew and ethnic Jews are expected to check their normative Jewish life and identity at the door.[20]

Wright's third-race theology does not merely reflect a lack of commitment to preserving a distinctive Jewish identity for the genealogical descendants of Abraham, Isaac, and Jacob. It also undermines Jewish presence in the church. We can see this reflected in Wright's vision for the expropriation, spiritualization, stigmatization, and deterritorialization of Jewish identity. I will give examples of each.

Expropriation. In Wright's dictionary, "fulfillment" means that non-Messianic Jews are the once-but-no-longer chosen folk. They have been disinherited from God's people, and their blessings have been transferred to the church: "In Romans 5–8 Paul argues that all of Israel's privileges have now been transferred, via the Messiah, to the worldwide people of God, the true family of Abraham."[21] Israel is now made up of Jews and gentiles who follow Jesus. Jews in the church are thus supposed to regard their Jewish family members and the wider Jewish community as faux Israel and former members of the people of God. Wright's teaching in this way divides *klal Yisrael* (all Israel) and alienates Jesus-believing Jews from their people. This destabilizes Jewish identity in the church.

Spiritualization. Wright maintains that all the privileges of Israel have been transferred to the church and that Christians are de facto Jews. As Wright puts it:

> For Paul anyone who was 'in the Messiah' and indwelt by the spirit could be called *Ioudaios* [Jew].[22]

---

20. Wright, *Paul and the Faithfulness of God*, 1443–44. There are no gentiles in Wright's third entity: "The Corinthians used to be 'gentiles' but are now no longer (12:2)" (1446).

21. N. T. Wright, "Justification: Its Relevance for Contemporary Evangelicalism (1980)," in *Pauline Perspectives: Essays on Paul, 1978–2013* (Minneapolis: Fortress, 2013), 32. Cf. Wright, *The Climax of the Covenant,* 250; Wright, *Paul and the Faithfulness of God*, 367–68. Expropriation in Wright's schema leaves room for the possibility that Jews can rejoin Israel through faith in Jesus and be saved.

22. Wright, *Paul and the Faithfulness of God*, 1444.

Those in the Messiah and indwelt by the spirit form the people
to whom Paul gives the word 'the Jew', 'the circumcision' and
even—if that reading is correct—'the Israel of God.'[23]

When this transference theology is embraced, Messiah-confessing
Jews cannot assert their Jewish identity without someone from a
non-Jewish background saying, "We are all Jews in the house of the
Lord!" Wright's theology thus creates an environment in which Jewish
followers of Jesus are excluded from having a unique covenantal identity in the church. This naturally results in assimilation and the loss
of Jewish presence.

Stigmatization. Wright's theology of Israel holds that Jews who
believe in Jesus are "weak" in faith if they observe Israel's dietary laws,
while eating *treif* (nonkosher food) is a sign of Christian "maturity."[24]
As Wright puts it, "it would appear not only that Paul was advising
gentile Christians in Corinth to eat nonkosher food but that he was
happy to see other 'Jewish Christians' following this pattern."[25] Wright
also describes keeping the Sabbath and Jewish festivals as "irrelevant"
and "a matter of 'indifference'" to Paul.[26] Circumcision is also repudiated: "Paul is indicating a messianic identity and way of life which
he sees as genuine worship of the God of Israel—only without circumcision and Torah-badges."[27]

Having served as a Messianic Jewish rabbi for over thirty years,
and having met many Christian pastors and Jews in churches, I can

---

23. Wright, *Paul and the Faithfulness of God*, 1107; cf. 539–41, 1147–48.

24. Wright, *Paul and the Faithfulness of God*, 1429, 1442. For a post-superses-
sionist interpretation of Rom 14, see David J. Rudolph, "Paul and the Food Laws:
A Reassessment of Romans 14:14, 20," in *Paul the Jew: A Conversation between
Pauline and Second Temple Scholars*, ed. Carlos A. Segovia and Gabriele Boccaccini
(Minneapolis: Fortress, 2016), 151–81; Tucker, *Reading Romans after Supersessionism*,
197–20.

25. Wright, *Paul and the Faithfulness of God*, 1429. Cf. 359.

26. Wright, *Paul and the Faithfulness of God*, 363–64, 1428.

27. Wright, *Paul and the Faithfulness of God*, 985–86, 1430.

attest that this indifference to Jewish difference is what is taught in churches and Bible studies where Wright's theology is embraced. But it goes beyond this. Wright maintains that Paul opposed the perpetuation of all boundary markers of Jewish identity:

> It was vital to Paul to see the Messiah's cross *blocking the way to any perpetuation of the world of Torah-observance* in which he had grown up and been active.[28]

> Paul is saying, as strongly as possible, that these identity-markers no longer matter.[29]

If Jewish boundary markers of identity no longer matter in God's kingdom, the implication is that God no longer desires Jews to live as Jews. Jewish life has has been superseded.[30] How do Jews in churches respond to this message? The evidence of more than fifteen centuries of church history indicates that when the church stigmatizes normative Jewish practice, Jews assimilate rather than perpetuate Jewish identity. From Wright's perspective, there is nothing wrong with this since Paul himself assimilated:

> And at this point some today might say, as some of [Paul's] contemporaries certainly did, that he had stopped being a 'Jew' altogether. He had abandoned the most basic markers of Jewish identity. So is that how he saw himself, too? Once more there are signals pointing in that direction.[31]

Given Wright's less-than-positive view of Jewish life, is it any wonder that his theology of Israel fosters the erasure of Jews in the body of Messiah? Pastors and churches that embrace this way of

---

28. Wright, *Paul and the Faithfulness of God*, 1433 (italics mine).

29. Wright, *Paul and the Faithfulness of God*, 1429n66; cf. 1430.

30. See David J. Rudolph, "The Science of Worship: Astronomy, Intercalation, and the Church's Dependence on the Jewish People," *Bulletin of Ecclesial Theology* 4.1 (2017): 41–46.

31. Wright, *Paul and the Faithfulness of God*, 1429.

thinking end up stigmatizing Jewish believers in Jesus who want to continue living out their Jewish identity. Wright's theology also implicitly encourages Jews in churches not to pass on Jewish identity to their children.

Deterritorialization. The land of Israel is central to Jewish identity (Gen 12:1–7).[32] In Wright's theology, however, God has universalized his promise to Abraham and the land of Israel is no longer a unique covenantal inheritance of the Jewish people. Wright explains:

> In Romans 4:13 Paul says, startlingly, "The promise to Abraham and his seed, that they should inherit the world." Surely the promises of inheritance were that Abraham's family would inherit the land of Israel, not the world? Paul's horizon, however, is bigger. The Land, like the Torah, was a temporary stage in the long purpose of the God of Abraham. *It was not a bad thing now done away with, but a good and necessary thing now fulfilled in Christ and the Spirit.* ... The Temple had been superseded by the Church. If this is so for the Temple, and in Romans 4 for the Land, then it must *a fortiori* be the case for Jerusalem. ... Jesus' whole claim is to do and be what the city and the temple were and did. As a result, both claims, the claim of Jesus and the claim of "holy land," can never be sustained simultaneously. ... The attempt to "carry over" some Old Testament promises about Jerusalem, the Land or the Temple for fulfilment in our own day has the same theological shape as the attempt in pre-Reformation Catholicism to think of Christ as being recrucified in every Mass. ... *The attempt to say that there are some parts of the Old Testament (relating to Jerusalem, Land or Temple) which have not yet been "fulfilled" and so need a historical and literal "fulfillment" now, or at some other time, is an explicit attempt to take something away from the achievement*

---

32. See Eugene Korn, *The Jewish Connection to Israel, the Promised Land: A Brief Introduction for Christians* (Woodstock: Jewish Lights, 2008), 3–11.

of Christ in his death and resurrection, and to reserve it for the work of human beings in a different time and place. The work of Christ is once again "incomplete." ... *The only appropriate attitude in subsequent generations towards Jews, the Temple, the Land or Jerusalem must be one of sorrow or pity.*[33]

Pastors who embrace Wright's fulfillment theology instruct Jewish members of their churches to view the land of Israel as no longer important to their identity, since it has been "fulfilled in Christ and the Spirit." This attempt to separate Jews from their land (deterritorialization) is one more way that Wright's theology of Israel undermines the Jewish identity of Jesus-believing Jews.

Wright regularly uses three terms to describe how the Messiah's mission impacted Israel and Jewish identity: *reworked, redefined,* and *fulfilled.* It is important to recognize that when Wright uses these words, as nice as they may sound to some Christian ears, he is implying expropriation, spiritualization, stigmatization, and deterritorialization of Jewish identity—all of which contribute to the erasure of Jews in the church. As Father Gregory Tatum puts it, "[Wright's

---

33. N. T. Wright, "Jerusalem in the New Testament," in *Jerusalem Past and Present in the Purposes of God,* ed. P. W. L. Walker (Cambridge: Tyndale House, 1992), 67, 70, 73–74 (italics mine); cf. Wright, *Paul and the Faithfulness of God,* 366–67. For a post-supersessionist interpretation of Rom 4:13, see David J. Rudolph, "Zionism in Pauline Literature: Does Paul Eliminate Particularity for Israel and the Land in His Portrayal of Salvation Available for All the World?" in *The New Christian Zionism: Fresh Perspectives on Israel and the Land,* ed. Gerald McDermott (Downers Grove, IL: InterVarsity, 2016), 167–94. For a post-supersessionist approach to the land of Israel in New Testament theology more generally, see Mark S. Kinzer, *Jerusalem Crucified, Jerusalem Risen: The Resurrected Messiah, the Jewish People, and the Land of Promise* (Eugene, OR: Cascade, 2018). Wright's argument assumes that, in Paul's thought, when something takes on new or additional meaning in Messiah, the fulfillment cancels out the validity of the prior practice or institution. However, Paul never puts forward this principle, and a number of texts call this criterion into question—e.g., marriage points to the relationship between Messiah and the church, yet marriage is not invalidated through the coming of Messiah (2 Cor 11:2; Eph 5:22–33). There is much in Paul's letters that envisions the universal and particular coexisting in God's kingdom, a view consistent with the eschatology of Israel's Scriptures.

eradication of Torah and his reinterpretation of Israel in which Israel-according-to-the-flesh ceases to be Israel in any meaningful sense] is not only an intellectual mistake, but from my perspective, morally unacceptable."[34] In sum, Wright's theology, when followed to its logical conclusion, leads to the erasure of the Jewish wing of the body of Messiah.

This brings us to the question of the degree to which this current book provides a platform for Wright's theology of Israel. In the next section I will aim to show how various elements of Wright's model that foster the erasure of Jews in the church show up in the essays by McKnight, Bird, and Witherington.

AN EVALUATION OF "PAULINE SUPERSESSIONISM"

More than a quarter of McKnight's essay is devoted to giving props to Wright's theology of Israel. McKnight describes Israel as "freshly reworked" (Wright's term), and he says that the best Christian scholarship uses the term "true" Israel to describe the "new" Israel (27). McKnight refers to "the one people of God, the church that is Israel expanded" (43), which seems to imply that non-Messianic Jews are not part of the people of God.

McKnight, who is not only a New Testament scholar but also a canon theologian in the Anglican Church in North America (ACNA), describes Messianic Jews as, "quite clearly in my judgment, resurrecting the debate Paul had with the Galatians and siding with the Judaizers to form two separate 'churches' in the one body of Christ" (15).[35] Here McKnight stigmatizes Messianic Jews because they want

---

34. Tatum, "Law and Covenant in *Paul and the Faithfulness of God*," 319 n. 15.

35. For a post-supersessionist interpretation of Gal 2:11–14, see David J. Rudolph, *A Jew to the Jews: Jewish Contours of Pauline Flexibility in 1 Corinthians 9:19-23* (Tübingen: Mohr Siebeck, 2011), 46–53; Magnus Zetterholm, "The Paul within Judaism Perspective," in *Perspectives on Paul: Five Views*, ed. Scot McKnight and B. J. Oropeza (Grand Rapids: Baker Academic, 2020), 180–82.

to retain Jewish communal life and practice[36] and insinuates that Messianic Jews promote judaizing.[37] Would a Jew in an ACNA church feel encouraged to retain Jewish identity given this kind of messaging?

---

36. Messianic Jewish communal life and identity is normative in the New Testament (Acts 15; 21:17–26; Matt 5:17–20; 1 Cor 7:17–24). See David J. Rudolph, "Messianic Judaism in Antiquity and in the Modern Era," in *Introduction to Messianic Judaism: Its Ecclesial Context and Biblical Foundations*, ed. David J. Rudolph and Joel Willitts (Grand Rapids: Zondervan, 2013), 21–36; Edwin K. Broadhead, *Jewish Ways of Following Jesus: Redrawing the Religious Map of Antiquity* (Tübingen: Mohr Siebeck, 2010), 80–160; David J. Rudolph, "Paul's 'Rule in All the Churches' (1 Cor 7:17–24) and Torah-Defined Ecclesiological Variegation," *Studies in Christian-Jewish Relations* 5 (2010): 1–23; David J. Rudolph, "Luke's Portrait of Paul in Acts 21:17–26," in *The Early Reception of Paul the Second Temple Jew: Text, Narrative and Reception History*, ed. Isaac W. Oliver and Gabriele Boccaccini with Joshua Scott (London: T&T Clark, 2018), 192–205; David J. Rudolph, "Was Paul Championing a New Freedom from—or End to—Jewish Law?" in *Understanding the Jewish Roots of Christianity: Biblical, Theological, and Historical Essays on the Relationship Between Christianity and Judaism*, ed. Gerald McDermott (Bellingham: Lexham, 2021); Matthew Thiessen, *Jesus and the Forces of Death: The Gospels' Portrayal of Ritual Impurity Within First-Century Judaism* (Grand Rapids: Baker Academic, 2020), 177–95; Daniel Boyarin, "Jesus Kept Kosher," in *The Jewish Gospels: The Story of the Jewish Christ* (New York: New Press, 2012), 102–28; David J. Rudolph, "Jesus and the Food Laws: A Reassessment of Mark 7:19b," *Evangelical Quarterly* 74.4 (2002): 291–311. For a window into contemporary Messianic synagogue life, see David J. Rudolph, "Contemporary Judeo-Christian Communities in the Jewish Diaspora," in *Encyclopedia of the Jewish Diaspora: Origins, Experiences, and Culture*, ed. M. Avrum Ehrlich (Santa Barbara, CA: ABC-CLIO, 2008), 1:146–50; David J. Rudolph and Elliot Klayman, "Messianic Synagogues," in *Introduction to Messianic Judaism*, 37–50; Seth N. Klayman, "Messianic Jewish Worship and Prayer," in *Introduction to Messianic Judaism*, 51–60.

37. In the opening essay of the present book, McKnight also writes that "post-supersessionist messianic Jewish thinkers … both resurrect the so-called judaizing wing of the letter of Paul to the Galatians and creates a massive fissure in the one people of God, the church that is Israel expanded" (43). For a more accurate view of Messianic Jews, see Daniel C. Juster, "Messianic Jews and the Gentile Christian World," in *Introduction to Messianic Judaism*, 136–44; Mark S. Kinzer, *Postmissionary Messianic Judaism: Redefining Christian Engagement with the Jewish People* (Grand Rapids: Brazos, 2005), 151–79; Mark S. Kinzer, *Searching Her Own Mystery: Nostra Aetate, the Jewish People, and the Identity of the Church* (Eugene, OR: Cascade, 2015), 1–24, 40–60. For scholarship on Messianic Jews and Messianic Judaism, see https://www.messianicstudies.com.

McKnight also portrays Messianic Jews as people who "are forming separate, segregated churches" (43),[38] even though one would experience more table fellowship between Jews and gentiles in a Messianic synagogue than in the average ACNA church.[39]

In another comment, McKnight goes further and argues that the Messianic Jewish congregational movement should be shut down and Messianic Jews should join local churches that reflect *third-race* fellowships:

> Wright sees a "third race" in the church, while Kinzer finds two kinds of church. I am closest, then, to Wright. I see the church as Israel expanded (and fulfilled, and therefore a new people with deep dimensions of continuity) in which Jewish believers will remain sometimes Torah-observant and gentile believers not Torah-observant except in general, but that they will form one fellowship—and I mean one local church that worships, teaches, and eats together—and will share the table together (kosher folks eating with non-kosher folks, and

---

38. It is not clear if McKnight also opposes Black churches, Hispanic churches, Korean churches, etc.

39. Gentile believers typically comprise more than half of the membership of Messianic congregations. Kinzer's bilateral ecclesiology is more of a theoretical model that reflects Jewish covenantal and communal realities than the normative demographic experience of Messianic synagogues. Kinzer makes room in his ecclesial vision for Jews in Christian churches when they adopt a progressive, pragmatic, and personal approach to Torah practice. See Mark S. Kinzer, "The Torah and Jews in the Christian Church—Covenant Calling and Pragmatic Practice" (paper presented at the Helsinki Consultation on Jewish Continuity in the Body of Messiah, Berlin, 2012), 1–13. From Kinzer's perspective, Messianic synagogues and Jews in churches are not either/or but both/and. Kinzer and I are actively involved in *Yachad BeYeshua* (Together in Jesus), an international fellowship of Jewish disciples of Jesus that includes Messianic Jews and Jewish members of Catholic, Orthodox, Protestant, and independent churches. See www.yachad-beyeshua.org. These Jewish Christians relate firsthand how difficult it is to identify as Jews, live out Jewish life, and pass on Jewish identity to their children when their churches promote a type of supersessionism similar to what Wright and the primary essayists of this book are advocating.

sometimes kosher folks not eating kosher). Thus, I agree with Wright that Jews and gentiles will *sit in mixed table fellowship* and so transcend difference in a new-creation kind of unity through the power of the Spirit. I agree, too, with Wright that "fulfillment in Christ" marks the new identity more than anything else. That there is neither Jew nor Greek in Christ means those ethnic identities will lead not to separation but to ethnicity-transcending *koinonia* at the table. (40) [40]

McKnight remarks later that "gentile believers have no right to diminish Israel (or Jews)" (42). However, is McKnight being respectful of Messianic Jews when he suggests that they should leave their synagogues, join predominantly gentile churches, eat nonkosher food, and not make a fuss when they can't keep all of their Jewish customs in the local church?[41]

Turning to Bird, he quotes Wright six times, uses the expression "Israel is redefined" (e.g., 46), and in various ways promotes a Pauline vision for the erasure of Jewish identity, such as when he approvingly cites Daniel Harlow as saying, "For Paul: *only those in Christ are in the covenant and among the elect. In his vision of a new humanity destined for a new creation, ethnicity—so essential to Jewish identity—disappears.* If this theology implies no wholesale rejection or supersession of Israel, it does imply a new definition of 'Israel.' "[42]

---

40. McKnight unpacks his case for a third-race view in Scot McKnight, "Saints Re-formed: The Extension and Expansion of *hagios* in Paul," in *One God, One People, One Future: Essays in Honor of N. T. Wright* (Minneapolis: Fortress, 2018), 211–13.

41. The Toward Jerusalem Council II Seven Affirmations (www.tjcii.org) represent an alternative way of viewing Messianic synagogues and Jews in churches that is more in line with respect for Jew-gentile diversity in the body of Messiah.

42. Daniel C. Harlow, "Early Judaism and Early Christianity," in *Early Judaism: A Comprehensive Overview*, ed. John J. Collins and Daniel C. Harlow (Grand Rapids: Eerdmans, 2012), 405 (italics mine). For Bird's citation in the present volume, see 50n13.

Bird advocates for a third-race ecclesiology when he writes that Paul's "Christ-believing groups are neither Jews nor pagans but rather the 'assembly of God,' a prestigious group with a privileged relationship with Israel's God through Christ (1 Cor 10:32)" (58).[43] In a footnote, Bird cites his own work, *An Anomalous Jew*, in which he says that "it seems hard to avoid the conclusion that Paul conceived of Christ-believers as a τρίτον γένος, or *tertium genus*: a third race."[44] Bird clarifies that his view is not a replacement theology. However, any ecclesial theology that fosters the erasure of Jews, especially when driven by a third-race vision, will ipso facto lead to a de facto all-gentile church. This has been the case for more than fifteen hundred years.[45]

Consistent with this trajectory, Bird concurs with Wright that Paul repudiated circumcision as a sign of God's covenant relationship with the Jewish people and universalized its meaning: "Circumcision is nullified (1 Cor 7:19; Gal 5:6; 6:15) and reinterpreted (Rom 2:25–29; Phil 3:3) as a marker of belonging to God's people" (58).[46] Like

---

43. For a post-supersessionist interpretation of 1 Cor 10:32, see Rudolph, *A Jew to the Jews*, 33–35; J. Brian Tucker, "Gentiles Identifying with Moses and Israel's Story in 1 Cor 10:1–13: Evaluating Aspects of the Wright-Hays Interpretive Framework," in *The Message of Paul the Apostle within Second Temple Judaism*, ed. František Ábe (Lanham: Lexington/Fortress Academic, 2020), 224–25.

44. Michael F. Bird, *An Anomalous Jew: Paul among Jews, Greeks, and Romans* (Grand Rapids: Eerdmans, 2016), 54. For this discussion in Bird's essay, see 46n44, where he also points to Wright's extended discussion of the third-race schema in *Paul and the Faithfulness of God*, 1443–49.

45. Jews in churches today tend to assimilate and not pass on Jewish identity to their children when their churches promote third-race theology. See Jonathan Allen, *A Profile of Jewish Believers in the UK Church* (Eugene: Wipf & Stock, 2018), 211–31; Antoine Lévy, *Jewish Church: A Catholic Approach to Messianic Judaism* (Lanham: Lexington, 2021). As an example of a church that is not third-race-oriented and is theologically committed to Jewish continuity, see Gateway Church (www.gateway-people.com) and the Gateway Center for Israel (www.centerforisrael.com).

46. For a post-supersessionist interpretation of 1 Cor 7:19, Gal 5:6, 6:15, Rom 2:25–29 and Phil 3:2–11, see Rudolph, *A Jew to the Jews*, 28–30, 44–46, 73–74; Tucker, *Reading Romans after Supersessionism*, 45–57; Christopher Zoccali, *Reading Philippians after Supersessionism: Jews, Gentiles, and Covenant Identity* (Eugene: Cascade, 2017),

Wright, Bird regards gentile Christians as spiritual Jews who take on the identity of Israel:

> For Paul, "Israel" is a prestige label for the superordinate group comprised of Christ-believing Jews and gentiles, who can be described elsewhere as an "inward Jew" (Rom 2:29), "children of the living God" (Rom 9:26), the "circumcision" (Phil 3:3), and the "Israel of God" (Gal 6:16). (59)[47]

In his conclusion, Bird writes, "Paul's messianic eschatology leads to viewing Israel as not replaced but expanded to include Christ-believing gentiles, so that Paul can simultaneously affirm that the distinction between Jews and gentiles is negated even as he retains a place for ethnic Israel in God's purposes" (63). From my perspective, the weak link in Bird's theology of Israel is that Jews and gentiles cease to be Jews and gentiles in any meaningful sense. He does not seem to view the church fundamentally as a table fellowship of Jews and gentiles in Messiah who are called to affirm one another

---

86–108, 131–36; Mark D. Nanos, "Paul's Polemic in Philippians 3 as Jewish-Subgroup Vilification of Local Non-Jewish Cultic and Philosophical Alternatives," in *Reading Corinthians and Philippians within Judaism, vol. 4 of Collected Essays of Mark D. Nanos* (Eugene: Cascade, 2017), 142–91.

47. Bird overstates the evidence for Paul including gentile believers in the term "Israel of God" (Gal 6:16). Of the seventy-seven times that "Israel" appears in the New Testament, seventy-six times it contextually refers to the Jewish people or land of Israel. Setting aside Wright's strained interpretation of Rom 11:26, there is only one instance where the meaning of Israel is in doubt—Gal 6:16. Here "Israel of God" may refer to *klal Yisrael* (the Jewish people), the faithful Jewish remnant, a subgroup of Jewish Christ-followers from Jerusalem, or Israel (without expropriation) and its eschatologically extended commonwealth. See Ralph J. Korner, *The Origin and Meaning of Ekklēsia in the Early Jesus Movement* (Leiden: Brill, 2017), 221–29; Gerald R. McDermott, *Israel Matters: Why Christians Must Think Differently about the People and the Land* (Grand Rapids: Brazos, 2017), 26–28; Susan G. Eastman, "Israel and the Mercy of God: A Re-reading of Galatians 6:16 and Romans 9–11," *New Testament Studies* 56.3 (2010): 367–95; Hans Dieter Betz, *Galatians: A Commentary on Paul's Letter to the Churches in Galatia* (Philadelphia: Fortress, 1979), 323; Peter Richardson, *Israel in the Apostolic Church* (Cambridge: Cambridge University Press, 1969), 82–83.

in their respective identities as Jews and gentiles and relate to each other in a spirit of interdependence, mutual blessing, and mutual humbling (Rom 11, 15; Eph 2).[48] Bird's third-race theology effectively undermines this Pauline vision. Bird offers no indication that Jewish believers in Jesus are called to remain practicing Jews in third-race communities that appropriate Israelite identity. The thrust of his essay is in line with Wright's redefined Israel and the various ways that it fosters the erasure of Jews in the church through expropriation and spiritualization of Jewish identity.

Witherington is the only author in the volume who does not follow the lead of Wright's model. Contrary to Wright, Witherington argues that when Paul uses the term "Israel" he means Jewish people. At the same time, Witherington seems to promote expropriation. As he puts it, "Furthermore, at any one moment in human history since the Christ event, there was only one people of God, with Jew and gentile united in Christ" (77). The implication is that Jewish people who do not believe in Jesus are no longer part of the people of God, though he believes they can return.

Like McKnight, Witherington draws on Galatians to stigmatize Messianic Jews. He describes Jesus-believing Jews who keep God's commandments specific to Israel (e.g., circumcision, Israel's festivals, dietary laws, etc.) as "tantamount to submitting again to bondage and renouncing the gospel of Christ and the new covenant he instituted" (74).[49] This negative Jewish messaging communicates to Jews

---

48. The author of Ephesians uses nuanced language to describe the relationship of gentile believers to Israel (*politeias tou Israel* ["commonwealth of Israel"], *amphoteroi* ["both"], *sun-/sum-/sus-* ["co-" prefixes], and the second-person plural pronoun and verb to identify gentiles in contrast to Jews); see Eph 2:11–22; 3:1, 5–6. The author thereby avoids giving the impression that the church is coterminous with Israel or that Jewish identity is erased or expropriated.

49. For a post-supersessionist interpretation of Gal 4:9–10, see Neil Martin, *Regression in Galatians: Paul and the Gentile Response to Jewish Law* (Tübingen: Mohr Siebeck, 2020); Kathy Ehrensperger, "Trouble in Galatia: What Should be Cut? (On Gal 5:12)," in *The Message of Paul the Apostle within Second Temple Judaism*, 180; Matthew Thiessen, *Paul and the Gentile Problem* (Oxford: Oxford University Press,

in churches that they should assimilate. In Witherington's theological vision, all of Jewish life is superfluous in Christ, including boundary markers of Jewish identity. The Torah had a "temporal and temporary function" (71) and has been "fulfilled" (i.e., "its day and time had come and gone"; 73).

Several times Witherington comments that in Paul's view Jesus-believing Jews can practice Jewish customs if the purpose is "to reach more Jews for Christ" (71). But wouldn't this make Messianic Jews inauthentic, chameleon-like, and deceptive?[50] Doesn't it also imply that Jews are simpletons who cannot see through this pretense? There are alternative post-supersessionist ways of understanding Paul's principle of flexibility in 1 Corinthians 9:19–23 that are more ethical and halakic in approach, but Witherington does not engage them.[51] In the end, Witherington falls in line with Wright, McKnight, and Bird in advocating for a kind of supersessionism that fosters the erasure of Jews in the church.

POST-SUPERSESSIONIST THEOLOGY

McKnight claims that post-supersessionist theology is rooted in religious pluralism and a lack of critical scholarship. This is wide of the mark in my opinion and is itself suggestive of McKnight's uncritical acceptance of a tendentious tradition and his lack of engagement

---

2016), 156; Justin K. Hardin, *Galatians and the Imperial Cult: A Critical Analysis of the First-Century Social Context of Paul's Letter* (Tübingen: Mohr Siebeck, 2008), 116–47; Mark D. Nanos, *The Irony of Galatians: Paul's Letter in First-Century Context* (Minneapolis: Fortress, 2002), 267–71.

50. See Rudolph, *A Jew to the Jews*, 12–13, 67–73; Mark D. Nanos, "Was Paul a 'Liar' for the Gospel? The Case for a New Interpretation of Paul's 'Becoming Everything to Everyone' in 1 Corinthians 9:19–23," in *Reading Corinthians and Philippians within Judaism*, 93–108.

51. For a post-supersessionist interpretation of 1 Cor 9:19–23 that is more in line with the context of 1 Cor 8:1–11:1, see Rudolph, *A Jew to the Jews*, 173–212; Matthew V. Novenson, "Did Paul Abandon Either Judaism or Monotheism?" in *The New Cambridge Companion to St. Paul*, ed. Bruce W. Longenecker (Cambridge: Cambridge University Press, 2020), 245.

with opposing scholarship.[52] The Society for Post-Supersessionist
Theology (www.spostst.org) defines its mission as follows:

> The Society for Post-Supersessionist Theology exists in order
> to promote research and discussion that advances post-su-
> persessionist thought. The Society understands post-super-
> sessionism as a family of theological perspectives that affirms
> God's irrevocable covenant with the Jewish people as a central
> and coherent part of ecclesial teaching. It seeks to overcome
> understandings of the New Covenant that entail the abrogation
> or obsolescence of God's covenant with the Jewish people, of
> the Torah as a demarcator of Jewish communal identity, or of
> the Jewish people themselves.
>
> The Society welcomes participation from all who seek to
> advance post-supersessionist theology. It especially seeks to
> promote perspectives that remain faithful to core Christological
> convictions; that affirm the ecclesia's identity as a table fellow-
> ship of Jews and gentiles united in the Messiah; and that engage
> with Jewish thought and tradition as an expression of ecclesial
> partnership with the Jewish people as a whole.

The founding members of the society include R. Kendall Soulen,
Mark Kinzer, David Rudolph, Holly Taylor Coolman, Gerald
McDermott, William Abraham, Gary Anderson, Craig Blaising,
Jeroen Bol, Ellen Charry, Gavin D'Costa, Tommy Givens, Justin
Hardin, Douglas Harink, Stanley Hauerwas, Kevin Hughes, George
Hunsinger, Willie Jennings, Craig Keener, Joseph Mangina, Ephraim
Radner, Anders Runesson, Katherine Sonderegger, J. Brian Tucker,
Pim Valkenberg, Tom Weinandy, and Joel Willitts. This diverse group
of gentile Christian and Messianic Jewish scholars is reflective of the
membership as a whole.

---

52. See www.post-supersessionism.com for the breadth of critical (including
confessional) scholarship being published in this field.

Similarly, the New Testament after Supersessionism series, published by Cascade, reflects a high level of discourse among confessional scholars who are faithful to core christological convictions. Its editorial board includes two gentile Christians and a Messianic Jew. Among Paul-within-Judaism scholars in Society of Biblical Literature circles, the diversity extends to traditional Jews and those who are secular. Relatively few of the leading Paul-within-Judaism scholars in my experience hold a *Sonderweg* reading of Paul.[53]

CONCLUSION

There are various kinds of supersessionism. Some are benign and others harm the body of Messiah. Wright's version of supersessionism—the third-race theology promoted in this book—is the more pernicious kind because of its vision for the expropriation, spiritualization, stigmatization, and deterritorialization of Jewish identity, which leads to the erasure of Jews in the church. All three essays in this volume include elements of this assimilationist messaging found in Wright's theology of Israel.

While supersessionism has different meanings today and the term can be misused,[54] there is a place for recognizing what it originally

---

53. *Sonderweg* here refers to a special path of salvation for the Jewish people. I find religious pluralism more prevalent in Jewish-Christian relations settings, ironically a place where Messianic Jews are often excluded (e.g., the Council of Centers on Jewish-Christian Relations). See David J. Rudolph, "Messianic Jews and Christian Theology: Restoring an Historical Voice to the Contemporary Discussion," *Pro Ecclesia* 14.1 (2005): 58–84; David J. Rudolph, "To the Jew First: Paul's Vision for the Priority of Israel in the Life of the Church," *Kesher: A Journal of Messianic Judaism* 37 (2020): 11–25; Jennifer M. Rosner, "Messianic Jews and Jewish-Christian Dialogue," in *Introduction to Messianic Judaism*, 145–55; Jennifer M. Rosner, *Healing the Schism: Barth, Rosenzweig, and the New Jewish-Christian Encounter* (Minneapolis: Fortress, 2015), 293–300. For a discussion of Messianic Jewish soteriology, see Daniel C. Juster, "The Narrow Wider Hope," *Kesher: A Journal of Messianic Judaism* 22 (2008): 14–41; Mark S. Kinzer, "Final Destinies: Qualifications for Receiving an Eschatological Inheritance," *Kesher: A Journal of Messianic Judaism* 22 (2008): 87–119.

54. None of this justifies subverting the term "supersessionism" through logocide or semanticide as the essays in Part 1 of the present volume do. See John Wesley Young,

meant before it sprouted so many variations. In his monograph *Aquinas on Israel and the Church*, Matthew Tapie surveys the history of the term and articulates the heart of its meaning in Christianity's traditional theology of the Jewish people. He concludes, "*Supersessionism is the Christian claim that with the advent of Christ, Jewish Law is fulfilled and obsolete, with the result that God replaces Israel with the Church.*"[55]

What is so striking to me about Tapie's definition of classical supersessionism is how closely it fits the bill of what Wright argues for, which explains why Paula Fredriksen dubs Wright's view "classic, indeed deeply traditional supersessionism."[56] McKnight and Bird attempt to rebrand Wright's theology of Israel and contend that it is not a replacement theology. However, at the end of the day, what happens to Jewish people in third-race churches? Are they not assimilated into a community that is no longer Jew or Greek? As the saying goes, "If it looks like a duck, swims like a duck, and quacks like a duck, then it probably *is* a duck!"

What difference does it make whether this book promotes traditional supersessionism or not? It makes *all* the difference, because we empirically know the devastating impact this theology has had on the Jewish people over the last eighteen hundred years. With anti-Semitism on the rise around the world, it is more important than ever that the church learn from its past and not repeat the errors of yesterday. We need to know the kind of theology that stokes the flames of anti-Semitism in the church and nip it in the bud rather than normalize it.

Totalitarian Language: Orwell's Newspeak and Its Nazi and Communist Antecedents (Charlottesville: University Press of Virginia, 1991), 104–14.

55. Matthew A. Tapie, *Aquinas on Israel and the Church: The Question of Supersessionism in the Theology of Thomas Aquinas* (Eugene: Pickwick, 2014), 23–24 (italics original). Cf. Matthew Tapie, "Christ, Torah, and the Faithfulness of God: The Concept of Supersessionism in 'The Gifts and the Calling,'" *Studies in Christian-Jewish Relations* 12.1 (2017): 1–18.

56. Fredriksen, review of *Paul and the Faithfulness of God* (by Wright), 389.

In many ways, Messianic Jews serve as the proverbial canary in the coal mine when it comes to detecting forms of supersessionism that are harmful. As Father Peter Hocken, a Catholic charismatic priest and one of the founders of Toward Jerusalem Council II,[57] puts it, "Encountering Messianic Jews is a challenging experience for any gentile Christian. We may be aware that much of the Christian world has begun to move away from the view that the church has replaced Israel as God's covenanted people. ... But often this remains a rather theoretical consideration remote from the burning theological issues of the day. Meeting Messianic Jews confronts gentile Christians with Jewish believers in Jesus who refuse to be 'replaced.' It faces Christians not just with a different theology but with an incarnate reality."[58]

---

57. See www.tjcii.org.

58. Peter Hocken, *The Challenges of the Pentecostal, Charismatic and Messianic Jewish Movements: The Tensions of the Spirit* (Burlington: Ashgate, 2009), 16. In a more recent article, Hocken writes: "For centuries converted Jews were simply assimilated into a Christian church, whether the Catholic, the Orthodox, or one of the Protestant churches. The distinctions that remained or arose within the church world did not include that between Jew and gentile. Thus the appearance of Messianic Jews who claim a distinct identity as Jewish disciples of Jesus, presents a huge challenge to all Christian theologies of church. The challenge is not just to find a place for the Messianic Jews, a slot into which the churches can fit them. The challenge to the gentiles is first to undo all the consequences of replacement thinking that either replaced Israel by the church or subsumed Israel into the church; the challenge is to restore the corporate Jewish witness to Yeshua to its rightful and foundational place within the body of Christ-Messiah. This can be the only authentic way to the healing of our divisions and to the manifestation of the unity of the one body. I see all of us gentile believers as beginners and learners in responding to the challenges raised by the Messianic Jews" (Peter Hocken, "Continuity and Discontinuity in the Relation of the Church to Israel," in *Azusa, Rome, and Zion: Pentecostal Faith, Catholic Reform, and Jewish Roots* [Eugene: Pickwick, 2016], 133–34).

PAUL, *NOSTRA AETATE*, AND IRREVOCABLE GIFTS IN LIGHT OF ROMANS' PLANT METAPHOR

JANELLE PETERS

During my undergraduate years, I had two rabbis as campus life and honors thesis advisors. Neither wanted to form their Judaism in the image of Christianity. One regaled me with tales of dreaming in Aramaic (rather than in Hebrew), while the other responded to my statement of my envisioned honors thesis topic of Jesus's crucifixion and resurrection with the query: "What about the Dead Sea Scrolls?" And so, I slogged through the dual messianic vision of the Essenes at Qumran. I neglected the person to whom Mary is said to have cried "Rabboni!" (John 20:16) in Hebrew, though it was actually Aramaic; there were no exclamations of "Rabboni" at Qumran. I turned away from the "Christ crucified" of Paul's letters in Greek; there was no Christ at Qumran, but there were *two* expected messiahs.

Nonetheless, since Paul's churches differ from the Judaism of Jesus and the Jerusalem apostles, this provides us a certain window into how Judaism was defined at the time. It shows us how followers of Christ were beginning to embark on a new so-called "way" that proponents of the "two ways that never parted" see. As Scot McKnight, Michael Bird, and Ben Witherington have all indicated, this illumination comes at the price of Paul prioritizing Christ before anything else in Judaism. This means that where the Torah and Christ diverge,

Christ-followers follow Christ and not the Torah. It is hard to see how Judaism can be respected as eternally valid if the Torah is not upheld. Yet the definition of Judaism as based on the Torah derives in part from Paul himself. And the fact that he does construct a Christ-following identity that can be distinct from his contemporary Judaism means that we have a rather progressive portrait of the Judaism of Jesus's ministry. Even those who were slow to understand Jesus's significance as Messiah seem to have accepted mixed-gender gatherings, a concern for the poor, and an emphasis on including prominent women in yeshiva and commensal settings. Paul also shared this social vision. We perhaps ask for too much when we expect Paul to have figured out how Judaism and Christianity could make universal claims without canceling each other out or needing to be ranked. Even the postmodern era hasn't figured out how to put Moses and Jesus in the same place at the same time; it's against the law of modern physics.

Since the Second Vatican Council, Catholic theology has moved toward creating a polity that resembles rabbinic literature by including the opinion of the minority on community decisions. With documents such as *Nostra Aetate*, *Lumen Gentium*, and others, Catholics have worked toward repairing their relationship with Judaism—a relationship that had been damaged not only by the tragic inaction on the part of some Catholic bishops during the Shoah, but also by nineteenth-century instances of Jewish children being baptized by their Catholic relatives and neighbors.[1] In 2015, in a document titled after Romans 11:29 (*The Gifts and the Calling of God are Irrevocable*), the Vatican set to correct the Good Friday liturgy that, as late as a 1960, blamed historical Jews for the death of Jesus.[2] Catholic theol-

---

1. Todd M. Endelman, "Jewish Converts in Nineteenth-Century Warsaw: A Quantitative Analysis," *Jewish Social Studies* 4.1 (1997): 28–59.

2. Marianne Moyaert, " 'The Gifts and the Calling of God are Irrevocable' (Rom 11:29): A Theological Reflection," *Irish Theological Quarterly* 83.1 (2018): 24–43. See also *The Gifts and the Calling of God Are Irrevocable (Rom 11:29): A Reflection on Theological Questions Pertaining to Catholic-Jewish Relations on the Occasion of the 50th Anniversary of Nostra Aetate* (10 December 2015), Commission of the Holy See

ogy sets its central questions based on its own sacred Scripture and saints, meaning that dialogue inevitably becomes about Paul rather than Maimonides.[3]

In this essay, I will (1) give a brief overview of how Catholicism defined its relationship to Judaism by means of Romans 11, (2) discuss Paul as a founder figure and "apostle of the gentiles," and (3) examine Paul's grafted olive tree image in light of the comments by Michael Bird, Scot McKnight, and Ben Witherington. All three draw on the ideas of scholars such as Jon Levenson and N. T. Wright that Christianity resembles Qumran and other Jewish sects in its supersessionism.[4] Focusing on the comparison of the eternal plant made by Bird and in my honors thesis supervised by Jewish scholar David Goodblatt, I will insist that Paul's own Jewish background as a Pharisee is as important to the image as the edict of Claudius that could have sent Aquila and Prisca from Rome to Corinth as Jewish followers of Christ. The image of the eternal plant is not as negative as it appears at first glance, as it also suggests that even in Paul's day the church resorted to a fusion of Judaism and Christianity that was more effective as

---

for Religious Relations with the Jews, http://www.vatican.va/roman_curia/pontifi-cal_councils/chrstuni/relations-jews-docs/rc_pc_chrstuni_doc_20151210_ebrais-mo-nostra-aetate_en.html (hereafter cited as *Gifts*).

3. Dru Johnson has noted that Maimonides thinks not every ritual will be traceable to the Torah. See the chapter on "Ritualization: A Better Construct than Supersessionism" in Dru Johnson, *Knowledge by Ritual: A Biblical Prolegomenon to Sacramental Theology*, Journal of Theological Interpretation Supplement 13 (Philadelphia: Eisenbrauns, 2016), 206–19 (esp. 209).

4. Aharon Shemesh relates the separatist laws of Qumran toward other Jews to the (rabbinic) halakah that forbids accepting gifts from gentiles. See Aharon Shemesh, "The Origins of the Laws of Separatism: Qumran Literature and Rabbinic Halacha," *Revue de Qumrân* 18.2 (1997): 223–41. This halakah adds significance to the 2015 Vatican *Gifts*, given that Paul claims Jews receive gifts from God and the "gift" is prominent in works by Catholic theologians such as Jean-Luc Marion (who graciously allowed me to audit his "gift and givenness" class at the University of Chicago).

a tactic than a strategy.[5] This agrees with the 2015 Roman Catholic reading of Romans whereby the Jewish covenant cannot be revoked, whether or not Jews follow Christ.

CATHOLIC HERMENEUTICS

From a Catholic perspective, as Gavin D'Costa has observed, the unique and primary character of Judaism has been bolstered since *Nostra Aetate* and *Lumen Gentium*. Pope John Paul II referred to the "irrevocable gift" that the divine had made to Jews.[6] Although D'Costa has pointed out that *Lumen Gentium* and accompanying documents seem to include Islam along with Judaism as believers in the same "one God" as Christians, it should be noted that Pope Benedict XVI's work on Jesus as a historical figure emphasizes the early Jewish context from which Jesus emerged. Catholicism inherently has an emphasis on the real: Catholics believe Jesus to be a real person who died a real death and experienced a real resurrection with the result that his body and blood are actually present in the celebration of Communion. Jews who do not follow Christ do not believe in the resurrection and transubstantiation; Muslims, by contrast, do not believe in the death of Jesus on the cross. The papal emphasis on Jesus as a historical person of Jewish heritage who died in Israel by order of the Roman governor has the effect of sometimes creating a static Judaism that is closer, but less finished, than the Christian movement that came later to create a new "way."

In order to eradicate pre-1960 theology on Jewish involvement in Good Friday, the Vatican has given direct statements on the need to not evangelize Jews in the wake of the Shoah. As D'Costa has noted, the idea of *Gifts* that the Jewish covenant was not revoked began

---

5. As Bruce Longenecker has noted, "perhaps the Pauline contribution lies less in the area of 'theology' and more in the area of practice—especially in the relation to his concern for the poor." Bruce Longenecker, "On Israel's God and God's Israel: Assessing Supersessionism in Paul," *Journal of Theological Studies* 58.1 (2007): 43.

6. Gavin D'Costa, "Supersessionism: Harsh, Mild or Gone For Good?," *European Judaism: A Journal for the New Europe* 50.1 (2017): 99–107.

with Pope John Paul II in 1980,[7] needed confirmation by the 1993 Catechism of the Catholic Church ("The Old Covenant has never been revoked"),[8] and was still new in 2015 with its connection to Romans 11. It is not insignificant that this Paul is very much being read in the present, not in the eschatological future.

To concentrate on Paul as the founder figure who led Christianity away from Judaism is to ignore the positive view of Judaism from Paul-oriented works such as 1 Clement. Although Paul definitively proves that some followers of Christ abandoned keeping kosher before the fall of the Second Temple, these early texts mention the temple sacrifices and the major heroes and heroines of the Hebrew Bible. They also lack any language of rebuke toward Pharisees or Sadducees. It is not the case that Paul causes a breach between former Judaism and future Christianity, even within his own circles within the early Christ-follower movement.

PAUL'S GREEN THUMB

The reason that supersession comes up is because Paul has to choose. After Jesus's resurrection, Paul resists the new movement and then himself converts to it. Then, as if to make up for his past persecution of Christ, he goes to the diaspora to preach the gospel. In explaining how the Jewish Jesus can be followed by gentiles without converting by circumcision, Paul has to narrate the relationship between Judaism in all of its other (not necessarily previous) forms and the movement centered on the person of Jesus as the risen son of God for all. He faces competition from rival ministers who would have gentiles circumcised to more formally convert to Judaism in order to follow Christ.[9] Even

---

7. *Gifts*, paragraph 39.

8. *Catechism of the Catholic Church*, 2nd ed. (Vatican: Libreria Editrice Vaticana, 2012), paragraph 121.

9. Paula Fredriksen explores some options in contemporary Jewish authors for the range of "Judaizing." See Paula Fredriksen, *Paul: The Pagan's Apostle* (New Haven: Yale University Press, 2017), 57–59.

though Paul claims we know now only in part, he takes horticultural imagery from contemporary Judaism and Roman literature to manufacture an image that forces Jews and gentiles to belong to the same discrete object. Imagine what would have happened if Paul had had network theory and the idea of "the cloud"! It might make clearer the "mystery" in Colossians to which McKnight gestures: "But for the Paul of Colossians the ecclesia is a profoundly new mixing of Jews and gentiles, something Paul calls the mystery—a mystery established on the basis of Christology, a Christology expressed in a soteriology, what I am calling a salvific supersessionism" (44).[10]

Paul's plant image in Romans is less supersessionist than the "mystery" of Colossians, which could be evidence that Paul the Pharisee is indeed more present in Romans than Colossians. The vision Paul has is of a root that is Israel and that forms the basis for newer, fresher grafts of the same species—olive branches. There is an echo of Paul's language of all body parts needing one another, but Paul nonetheless has to flatter his audience; they may consider themselves better than the original root and must keep this superiority to themselves.

As Bird notes, the grafted olive tree of Romans can be read as having some harmony with the Dead Sea Scrolls. While supervising my honors thesis, David Goodblatt suggested to me that the Qumran community saw itself as the flowering of the eschatological plant.[11] The imagery of this everlasting plant runs throughout the Scrolls, as does a general motif of horticulturally based language.[12] It connects with the classic Jewish hope of the restoration of the Davidic monarchy in the land of Israel voiced in the book of Isaiah, especially 60:21 and 61:1–3. Through the image of the plant, Hodayot[a] clearly shows the way the future elevated community will bring about the political,

---

10. Page numbers in parentheses refer to the essays in Part 1 of the present volume.

11. This received high honors in 2002 at the University of California, San Diego.

12. Patrick A. Tiller, "The 'Eternal Planting' in the Dead Sea Scrolls," *Dead Sea Discoveries* 4.3 (1997): 312–35.

cosmic, and possibly temporal unity. Describing the condition of the members, Hodayot[a] 14.14–16 reads: "Their root will sprout like a flower of the field forever, to make a shoot grow in the branches of the everlasting plantation so that it covers all the world with its shade, and its crown reaches up to the skies, and its roots down to the abyss" (cf. 1QS 8.4–6). This is perhaps the full flowering of the plant mentioned in the Damascus Document, which is situated in Israel after the Babylonian Exile (CD 1.5–8).

At the same time, Paul uses grafting images very common in Roman literature of the time. If we compare contemporary Roman authors, we notice that Paul lacks the sophistication of using techniques such as inarching (fusion instead of transplant) and grafting five to seven varieties on the same branch simply for the novelty.[13] It is almost as though Paul uses the image to draw attention to the facts that the catechetical timeline of the newly baptized might be years rather than weeks for his gentile congregants and that the varietals remain only two (Jew and non-Jew).

Bird notes an inherent inequality in Romans with Paul's idea that the church acts "as the shoot from the tree stump of Jesse, from which the whole tree would be renewed and sprout forth again" (61). While those in the Jewish community who do not believe in Christ are nonetheless fundamental to Paul's vision, the invigorating aspect in this metaphor comes from the gentiles. Paul, as an apostle to the gentiles, must surely advocate strongly for his chosen mission field. However, we must ask: Is Paul therefore also part of the root to be refreshed? How did Paul miraculously switch sides? Is this yet another example of Paul's self-debasement to flatter his audience?[14]

Bird's answer is that Paul gives a fundamental teaching: *extra Israel nulla salus*, "outside of Israel there is no salvation." However, Israel

---

13. Dustan Lowe, "The Symbolic Value of Grafting in Ancient Rome," *TAPA* 140.2 (2010): 461–88.

14. Janelle Peters, "Crowns in 1 Thessalonians, Philippians, and 1 Corinthians," *Biblica* 96.1 (2015): 67–84.

is not described as inviting gentiles to participate in Israel. Instead, God has allowed gentiles into Israel by grafting them in as an accommodation due to the "stumbling" of Israel for their failure to recognize the risen Christ as any messiah, let alone *the* Messiah. (Again, I should note that a singular leader does not follow the Mosaic leadership pattern of seeking support and consensus, and Jewish groups contemporary to Jesus could plausibly expect multiple messiahs just as they could expect both the return of Moses *and* Elijah at the transfiguration.) Thus, as Bird notes, Paul "effectively dissolved the in-between position of God-fearer" (58). There is also, I note, no Achior or Ruth—someone who is both a Jewish convert but also not an ethnic member of Israel but of some other nation. This would also mean that those of Italy do not get to differentiate themselves as members of advanced civilizations, given that they are all lumped together in a manner not unlike the cosmopolitan ideal of the Stoic global citizen. It is not simply Israel who is taking a subordinate role here; the individual regional identities—including Roman and barbarian—are being reconfigured as well.

What is interesting is that the idea of a nation is being obliterated by Paul precisely after a period that Steven Weitzman has argued saw the rise of Israel trying on ancient nationalism in order to compete with surrounding polities in wresting semiautonomous status from imperial powers.[15] This perhaps offers some pushback against David Novak's argument (cited by Bird) that "Christianity must be generically supersessionist" (62). If Paul's project in Romans is a dissolution of tribal identity on the part of his audience, then this might be another instance that is less about subordinating Israel than about engaging in conceptual play with the primal androgyne of the baptismal promise. This is especially compelling if the Romans knew

---

15. Steven Weitzman, "On the Political Relevance of Antiquity: A Response to David Goodblatt's *Elements of Ancient Jewish Nationalism*," *Jewish Social Studies* 14.3 (2008): 165–72.

about the expulsion of Jews such as Prisca and Aquila from Rome.[16] Paul must reassert Andronicus and Junia as apostolic leaders because they have been kept out of Roman house churches by the policies of Claudius. Like Paul, Jewish Christians may also be apostles. Jewish Christians are within both parts of Paul's grafted olive image. They are enlivening themselves. In this Roman context, the only polities for which Paul has eyes are Israel and the house churches of God.

There is also a sense in which the idea that Israel can be completely wrong and not be excluded from God is a positive. As Bird notes, the apostle goes into a cosmopolitan vein when he holds that Israel's errors led to "riches for the world" (Rom 11:12). Paul's statement that the gentile inclusion conveyed "reconciliation to the world" (11:15) suggests that Torah-observance has not been ruled out entirely. Without Christ, there would be no place for gentiles in God's plan, since Torah-observance sufficed and the inclusion comes about only because the Messiah needs to have believers (11:11, 31). Even though the root of Israel does not believe in Christ, they are still part of this grafted olive tree, because the gentiles possess correct belief while the Jews possess correct ritual and partial belief. Jewish Christians have correct ritual and correct belief, even though Paul does not commend circumcision for gentiles anywhere.

All metaphors have gaps. Likewise, within Judaism during the Second Temple period and rabbinical period, there is a conservational aspect. Even Qumran, which Bird notes was supersessionist within Judaism, demonstrates this well. Shemarayahu Talmon's analysis of the textual diversity of the Scrolls often is read as pointing to the tendency of Qumran to preserve many interpretations so as not to lose any inspiration, following a longstanding Jewish tradition to include divergent accounts that can be traced through to the Chronicler and the doublets of J and E material in the first books of the Hebrew scriptures—a notion that stands in sharp contrast to the later move

---

16. Wolfgang Wiefel, "The Jewish Community in Ancient Rome and the Origins of Roman Christianity," *Judaica* 26 (1970): 65–88.

within Jewish and Christian traditions to establish a list of canonical texts by which the others would then be deemed heterodox through the power dynamic of the process of naming.[17] John Collins notes that the "Dead Sea sect was heir to multiple traditions that were not strictly consistent to each other but were woven together nonetheless."[18] If Johannes van der Ploeg is correct, we have an example of the tendency to preserve and assemble various traditions in the War Scroll.[19] He surmises that it combines influences from Daniel 11— apparently not then perceived quite as an unalterable *textus receptus* by the community at Qumran—that described a holy war against the Kittim (the foreign powers dominating Israel) with a later conception of a forty-year war against the entire non-Israel world and with various rules concerning preparation and combat. Qumran is similar to Paul not only in being slightly supersessionist, but also in simply seeing all non-Jewish nations in the same category. Paul could be like Qumran in being ideologically inconsistent at times but with an aim toward the establishment of a community nonetheless.

As Ben Witherington pointed out in his essay, Paul must resemble Alan Segal's apostate Jew, and yet he keeps going back to the synagogue until he gets kicked out and lashed (2 Cor 11:24). Does this make Paul the Pharisee supersessionist against Qumran? As long as Paul is going to show up in places where he is on tenuous ground, why not with the Essenes? They both tend toward celibacy. Paul never singles out sects within Judaism like the Gospels do. He does not say Pharisaism is wrong; he says Israel has stumbled. The supersessionism of Paul might have a slightly different character, in that he actually is not naming the Pharisees in particular as wrong. Paul's

---

17. Shemaryahu Talmon, "The Old Testament Text," in *The Old Testament*, vol. 3 of *The Cambridge History of the Bible*, ed. P. R. Ackroyd and C. F. Evans (Cambridge: Cambridge, 1970), 159–99.

18. John J. Collins, *Apocalypticism in the Dead Sea Scrolls* (London: Routledge, 1997), 99.

19. Johannes van der Ploeg, *La rouleau de la guerre* (Leiden: Brill, 1959), 11–22.

main problems with Judaism create a sense of a unified Judaism for his audience; all of the sudden, this group that is in-fighting about the brass tacks of calendars and the resurrection has family traits that help identify it as a group—circumcision, kosher food, and the elevation of the Torah(s) given to Moses.

Given that we don't even need to reconstruct the leadership roles of Aquila, Prisca, Andronicus, and Junia after the end of Claudius's edict, because we have Paul the Pharisee firmly established, we should see the olive tree of Romans as having the same complexity as Paul.[20] It is correct to note that the olive tree has the aspect of critiquing the lack of acceptance among many Jews of Paul or Christ. Yet it inherently forces gentiles to accept Israel's primacy. If, as Witherington observes, Paul goes to the synagogues and *has the marks to show for it*, he seems not to keep strictly to his gentile mission. He has to go to the synagogues just like he has to explain how Christ can bring salvation despite contemporary understanding of the Torah. While he refers to the Stoics and even Menander, he is deeply committed to bringing the Jewish community along with him.

PAUL, THE PROBLEM

The real problem for Catholic-Jewish relations is not that Paul doesn't care about the Jews. He does. The real problem is that a theology that includes an Other only within its own frame of reference is not adequately seeking to understand the Other. If one is talking about eschatological plants at Qumran and within Judaism, for example, one could consider the angels also at Qumran. The angels at Qumran are within the community much like numinous beings in Japanese

---

20. Caroline Johnson Hodge has suggested the olive tree goes past the proselytism root-growth image of Philo (*Praem.* 152) to a "family tree." See Caroline Johnson Hodge, *If Sons, Then Heirs: A Study of Kinship and Ethnicity in the Letters of Paul* (Oxford: Oxford, 2007), 143. Such a genealogy would be necessary given Josephus's references to the public records kept at the Temple in *Contra Apionem* (I, 7) and *Vita* (I). See Jacob Z. Lauterbach, "The Three Books Found in the Temple at Jerusalem," *Jewish Quarterly Review* 8.4 (1918): 401.

anime or the book of Daniel. Sometimes they have political purposes; other times they are simply inhabiting the community and attending worship.[21] My teacher David Goodblatt believed that the accounts of angels were influenced by Persian and even possibly Buddhist influences; we see a rise in angelology and multitudinous bodhisattvas around this time. The angels were not guardian angels; they were not bad angels; they were not Watchers. They were angels in the community.[22]

The numinous quality of these angels was like that of a Torah scroll. Therefore, they were different from Catholic numinous objects such as the Eucharist. The Host creates sight lines that mandate the believer genuflect when crossing their paths. One parish where I went to Adoration had an angel to put in front of the Host when no one was there, so that Jesus's sight line would not be left unattended. The Eucharist also comes in two species—body and blood—which can be consumed by the believer. No one takes an angel like they take Communion. Although Paul speaks of being a spectacle for angels and of having angels at the Communion meal, Catholics do not routinely think beyond their guardian angels, archangels, or "all the angels and saints." Communion is a foretaste of the eschaton; Qumran's eternal plant, according to Goodblatt, could have been flowering with the angels in the community.

To simply loop Judaism into Catholicism elides some of these angels. Paul says we will judge angels (1 Cor 6:3), the 2003 Catholic

21. Esther G. Chazon, "Liturgical Communion with the Angels at Qumran," in *Sapiential, Liturgical and Poetical Texts from Qumran*, ed. Daniel K. Falk, Florentino Garcia Martinez, and Eileen M. Schuller (Leiden: Brill, 2000), 95–105.

22. On the other hand, angels in Jewish texts that did not make it into the Jewish canon but into the Catholic canon have been misconstrued as Catholic. Joseph A. Fitzmyer has observed that the Qumran Aramaic Tobit fragments answer the question of whether Raphael originally ate in the negative, meaning that the original version had not been Christianized as some claimed before Tobit was found at Qumran. Joseph A. Fitzmyer, "The Aramaic and Hebrew Fragments of Tobit from Qumran Cave 4," *Catholic Biblical Quarterly* 57.4 (1995): 664.

Catechism equates angels with divine benefactors,[23] and Qumran as a manifestation of Judaism had angels in their midst (1QH[a]). To impose a Catholic notion of angels on the Qumran angels would be to misunderstand the function of angels at Qumran.[24] It is probably only our desire to give Judaism essential qualities—rather than to see Judaism as diverging and converging from its offshoot of Christianity—that has led us to stereotype it as Pharisaic or Jerusalem-elite Judaism. Certainly, Goodblatt did not idolize Josephus any more than he idolized the scribes at Qumran; the group at Qumran and the groups associated with its texts preserved the plurality of thought of ancient Jews.[25] We must be careful: while noting the supersessionism of ancient Judaism as well as the Pauline churches, we must not use this as a license to restrict current Judaism to Pharisaic Judaism or to equate everything ascetical in current and Pharisaic Judaism with everything in Pauline ascetical and libertine house churches.[26]

Like Paul, the church should perhaps practice the virtue of showing up at the synagogue, even more so given the disproportionate control the church has over the globe. We are no longer in the world of first-century house churches. We must find out how Judaism is reinterpreting its received traditions again and again for each new moment. It is perhaps for the purposes of dialoguing with actual practitioners that recent studies of *Nostra Aetate* have emphasized the role Rabbi Abraham Heschel played in the Second Vatican Council. Heschel had friendships with several cardinals and advocated for the latest reform of the Roman Catholic Church to include statements on

---

23. Catechism of the Catholic Church, paragraph 350.

24. Esther G. Chazon, "Lowly to Lofty: The *Hodayot's* Use of Liturgical Traditions to Shape Sectarian Identity and Religious Experience," *Revue de Qumrân* 26.1 (2013): 3–19.

25. David Goodblatt, "Josephus on Parthian Babylonia (*Antiquities* XVIII, 310–379)," *Journal of the American Oriental Society* 107.4 (1987): 622.

26. Some Essenes might have married to continued the sect, according to Josephus (*War* 2.160–161). See Will Deming, *Paul on Marriage and Celibacy: The Hellenistic Background of 1 Corinthians 7* (Cambridge: Cambridge, 1995), 97.

the Church's relationship with the Jewish people.[27] That *Nostra Aetate* includes non-Catholic and non-Jewish religions could then mean that Heschel's vision was moving away from supersessionism, just as the Roman Catholic Church was attempting to become more inclusive. But the church cannot rely on a civil rights leader such as Heschel to be interested in Catholicism every generation. It must find ways of safeguarding the Jewish covenant without insisting that Judaism be brought within the church or vice versa, a fate none of my Jewish advisors has ever wanted.

In 2015, more progress was made in a statement that invoked Romans 11. Although the authors make convincing statements for Paul's supersessionism, the Vatican document *The Gifts and the Calling of God are Irrevocable (Rom 11:29)* advances the idea of the eternal promise of God's covenants with Israel and the Jewish people. Just as Jews may reinterpret ancient Jewish sects to include them within modern Judaism, Catholics may read Paul as being a more generous dispenser of salvation than would have happened in the past.

I will end with the conclusion of Walter Cardinal Kaspar in citing Martin Buber at a Cambridge talk on Jewish-Christian dialogue: "There is a way of unifying the prayers without unifying those who are praying."[28] Jews and Catholics believe in the same God of Israel, but the way they envision God giving covenants differs radically. Simply putting Paul within Judaism will be a stopgap measure for casual anti-Semitism on the part of churchgoers, but it ignores the real disagreements between Paul and the synagogues in which he debated. There was and is some supersession between forms of Judaism and Christianity, but that Catholics need not proselytize Jews means that Jews are saved with only the Jewish covenant. Although Paul, a former

---

27. Joshua Furnal, "Abraham Joshua Heschel and *Nostra Aetate*: Shaping the Catholic Reconsideration of Judaism during Vatican II," *Religions* 7.6 (2016): 70.

28. Walter Cardinal Kaspar, "The Relationship of the Old and the New Covenant as One of the Central Issues in Jewish-Christian Dialogue" (speech at the Centre for the Study of Jewish-Christian Relations, Cambridge, 6 December 2004).

Pharisee, couldn't resist engaging in dialogue with his former Jewish colleagues, the Roman Catholic Church must definitely not pressure Jews into following Christ. Jews have salvation on their own terms.

A CRITICAL RESPONSE TO PAULINE SUPERSESSIONISM

RONALD CHARLES

M y assigned role in this project is to offer a response to the essays in Part 1 of the volume. I will do so as someone trained in New Testament in a religious studies context of a research university. My teaching and research is within that particular context. I approach this difficult topic more from a position of description than investment in a religious tradition. I understand the highly sensitive nature of the topic, and I appreciate the fact that some scholars may be more invested in particular religious beliefs and activities than I am, as they perform their scholarship. I hope that despite my very critical response to the essays my colleagues will understand that I appreciate their work and that I have learned quite a lot from reading their contributions.

The first essay with which I will engage is that of Scot McKnight, "The Sport of Supersessionism: A Game to be Played." The contour of my response will be that of probing questions and reflections, moving from the introduction of the essay to its conclusion. The second essay with which I will engage is that of Michael Bird, "Paul's Messianic Eschatology and Supersessionism." I engage in a close reading of the text and push for closer examination of the data. The third and last essay is that of Ben Witherington, III, "Paul, Galatians, and Supersessionism." I show some of the weaknesses and contradictions in the essay while appreciating the level of complexity in the analysis.

MCKNIGHT: "THE SPORT
OF SUPERSESSIONISM"

In his introductory remarks, McKnight suggests that "the sport of supersessionism has become a bully club in the hands of some elites" (15). He offers that the bullies "put the bully club down long enough to admit reality" (15). Never in the essay does he identify any of the bullies. The so-called bullies, in McKnight's view, must cease to be delusional and must admit the reality that religious devotees of Judaism, Christianity, and Islam are "*inherently particularist*" (15; italics added). Otherwise, they would "diminish their faith with *pluralism*" (15; italics added). There are several difficulties with this stance. First, placing the myriad of followers of Judaism, Christianity, and Islam in one basket as being "inherently particularist" is problematic. McKnight does not qualify what he means by the term "inherently particularist." But how does he know that, if he means that the majority of devotees in these religious traditions adhere solely to their own theological conclusions? The statement is far from being specific, since there is not even one point proposed whereby one could focus and do a thorough examination. It could be clearer if he said it may be understandable that devotees of Judaism, Christianity, and Islam think that the religious tradition in which they engage is good. It is somewhat natural that one's identity will have boundaries that distinguish one's own religious activity from some other religious beliefs and activities. The question is: Is it necessary to denigrate some other religious tradition in order to experience a particular religious tradition to be good? Is it important, appropriate, or necessary for a person to consider their religious tradition to be *better*—perhaps in the form of *superseding* an earlier tradition?

There is, from the introduction, a serious lack of specificity related to the audience of the essay, its aim, and its methodology. The author does not indicate whether his focus is on the past—that is, on interpreting the New Testament texts in their historical, ideological, rhetorical settings—or whether his aim is to understand the theological significance of these texts for the contemporary context(s). McKnight seems to present himself as being part of a group he sees as "we orthodox" in contradistinction to another group or groups he sees as "the religious pluralists." These religious pluralists are perceived to be denouncing what the so-called or so-affirmed orthodox "really believe happened in history itself" (16). I confess I am a bit lost in this kind of reasoning. McKnight's aim is to present "an expansive sense of super-sessionism" in order to arrive at a particular "religious truth" (16). He continues his preliminary observations with two questions, that will direct his thoughts and conclusions—namely, first, "Is Christianity's belief in Jesus as God, or the Trinity, a sufficiently restrictive faith (or break) within Judaism to make most or many forms of contemporary Judaism uncomfortable?" (16), and, second, "Is belief in Jesus neces-sary for salvation for both Jews and gentiles?" (16).

To the first query, Christianity cannot believe in Jesus as God or the Trinity. There is no such thing as "Christianity" as divorced from actual people in times and spaces. People believe, whereas a religious system (Christianity) does not. The question could be asked differ-ently, in the sense of probing whether Christianity as a belief system could exist without people within that belief system believing that Jesus is necessary for salvation for both Jews and non-Jews. There are still difficulties with that, because the religious system that came to be known as Christianity in the early fourth century came from a rich tradition of debates about Jesus's divinity and the Trinity. The Nicene Creed and other "orthodox" creeds affirm these points, but various groups of Christians in the past—and in the present—have lived their Christian faith without adhering to the divinity of Christ or to the Trinity.

To the second question, there is a lack of clarity in the phras-ing. One may ask: What sort of belief in Jesus is necessary? What kind of salvation? Salvation for or from what? The author obviously has a contemporary and theological goal in mind, but that does not help his case for pushing one to answer the same way he does to the question: "How can one say Jesus is Messiah and not, at some level, be supersessionist in one's faith, in comparison to those who think Jesus is not Messiah?" (16). McKnight understands clearly the danger of a particularly destructive and anti-Semitic kind of supersessionism that diminishes the integrity of another person, especially in terms of that person's gender, race, and ethnicity. But he seems to understand the Bible as presenting a unifying and unproblematic view (at least from our own perspective in our time and place) about these complex issues. The Bible is not a depository of beautiful ways of understanding issues we grapple with today. What does "the Bible's narratival intent" really mean? The Bible has many things to say about many things and nothing to say about many others. There is not one "narratival intent." Rather, there are different goals—theological, rhetorical, political, literary, historical, and polemical/ideological goals—in the various texts of the Bible. Stating that is not turning "all truth claims into little more than personal, subjective, cultural, and historical preferences" (17). Truth claims are what they are. One needs to assert them critically and not think that one truth claim negates another truth claim. Certainly, we come to whatever we do or to whatever conclusion we hold with our own personal, subjective, intellectual, cultural, and historical penchant. McKnight comes to the texts and to his task in this essay as a male, white, American, Christian and conservative, privileged New Testament professor. Our place in the world does not preclude us from doing excellent work of scholarship, but we should not think or pretend that we approach our tasks devoid of presuppositions and personal, subjective, cultural, and historical preferences, whereas we think others do.

McKnight concludes his introduction with a quick (maybe too quick) glance at the so-called "parting of the ways" to dismiss the historical subtleties. How does mentioning that the parting happened advance his argument? In fact, what kind of argument(s) is he trying to make? It does not seem to be an argument that would help a reader understand the terms and social conditions of the first-century. His interest is in the question of truth, without explaining what kind of truth he is seeking to understand.

SETTING THE DEBATE

In setting the debate, McKnight has chosen to engage the works of two systematic theologians (one Methodist Christian, the other a Messianic, Christian/Jewish interpreter) and one New Testament scholar. One may wonder about the rationale of such choices.

The first point of observation is that McKnight never explains his choice of interlocutors. He does not indicate the audience of his essay, hence the confusion about what he is trying to do. He mentions Paul only briefly in this section, and the few Pauline texts mentioned (2 Cor 3:14; Rom 5:12–21; 9–11; Gal 3:15–4:7) are not given any proper exegesis. The mere mention of biblical verses to justify one's theological conclusion does not constitute appropriate arguments. Texts need to be excavated and explained within their specific contexts. McKnight places himself in a superior scholarly position to that of R. Kendall Soulen, who does "not interact with the *finest Christian studies*" (25; italics added). The disparaging tone with regard to Soulen's work continues unabated when McKnight states pontifically: "it is not quite as simple as Soulen presents it. Yes, to be sure, some use bold and simple strokes and virtually wipe out Israel but *the best of Christian scholarship is more nuanced* and finds a 'new' kind of Israel and a 'true' Israel as opposed to the balder sense that Israel was for the former days but now we have the (gentile) church'" (26; italics added). It seems to me that the bully, to use McKnight's image, is the one who devalues the work of others, such as Soulen, as portrayed to be so inferior to his own. It would be bolder for McKnight to go after the works of heavyweight New Testament scholars who present serious challenges to his theological deductions than to attack a systematic theologian like Soulen, who does his work as carefully as possible within the contours of his specific training. A question I have about the aforementioned quote is the following: Is "true" Israel opposed to a "false" Israel?

LAUDING THE WORKS OF A FELLOW SCHOLAR

Scholarship is certainly a communal enterprise. We learn from one another; we criticize one another; we sharpen one another's arguments. That is how we grow as scholars. However, it is rather strange that a scholar would praise another colleague as "*the* most significant New Testament scholar in the world today" (26; italics added). We are not members of a fan club. We may appreciate the contributions of others and even admire their works for various reasons, but the attitude of lauding a colleague to such an extent is one that is not called for. Thus, McKnight places N. T. Wright (a seasoned New Testament scholar) in the middle, as a kind of meat-of-resistance in a delicious theological sandwich, to savor his "salvific supersessionism." For several pages, the reader is exposed to long quotes from Wright, and in one instance Soulen is again attacked for having "completely missed" a point (29). Nowhere does a reader find McKnight's own thoughts. It is only lip service to critical engagement with Wright's work when McKnight states: "the point I want to make is not whether I agree with Wright but whether this is supersessionism (which Wright says it is— sectarian but not hard supersessionism) and what this looked like on the ground" (36). The section on Wright ends without McKnight's having said anything substantial. Zilch. Then he moves on to show the weakness of a Messianic Jewish theologian.

ESTABLISHING A POINT

In this section, McKnight engages with the work of Mark Kinzer. Clearly, he is no fan of Kinzer, especially when he considers Kinzer's two-covenants position. For McKnight—or "for many of us" (37), as he states without making clear who is included in this first-person plural pronoun—such a position is "the alarming part" (37). Then he makes a few claims, which remain unclear to me. Before he moves to establish his own point, he tries to show what the supportive elements of his position are. But the arguments are muddled. He states, "If I find separate churches unfaithful to the Pauline mission of churches marked by unity of all sorts (Gal 3:28), I do not do so by way of diminishing the reality of the Jewish identity of Messianic Jews. I celebrate that identity" (39).

I find the last section of the essay most helpful when McKnight presents his own understanding of the topic. He could have given the aim of the paper at the very beginning, instead of pretending to move "out of the realm of analogies and history and into theology" (39). That is what the paper has been all along! It would be useful to a reader if McKnight would elaborate a bit more, would move from claims to actual demonstration of arguments, and would be clearer with his assertions. It would be better for the reader if the issue of "truth—ultimate religious truth" (40) were driving the discussions. It would have been better to argue the content of the issue rather than presenting it as truth to be accepted. The "game" of truth, as the author dubbed it, is played on various terrains.

The author argues that "there is clearly a place for (ethnic) Israel in Paul's thought, ... but Paul knows they must believe in Jesus in order to inherit that promise" (41–42). The question is: How is it that an "expanded" Israel precludes any Israelites who do not believe in Jesus? How is that an expansion of Israel? How does that expansion honor the significance and the vitality of Judaism, both in the ancient and in the contemporary world?

It does not do to argue a case by merely reverting to John and quoting one of the "I am" statements (John 14:6), especially as the statement is not placed within its proper Johannine theological agenda. Alluding to Luther with "redemption alone" or "Jesus alone" works when preaching to the choir, but such rhetorical tropes do not touch skeptics or critical thinkers outside of a particular theological and conservative fold.

The conclusion to the essay is the weakest. It asserts that "the issue driving some of the supersessionistic accusations and the post-supersessionistic readings is pluralism—religious pluralism" (44). Embedded in this quote is labeling as Other anyone who is not in agreement with the author and branding pluralism and religious pluralism (never defined, explained, or clear as to what it entails in the contemporary world) as something to flee away from. Not once does McKnight even hint at some ways of engaging, and even affirming, one's religious tradition while living in a pluralistic world, respectful of and knowledgeable about other religious traditions.

I find the final question of the essay somewhat simplistic. Thinking of Jesus as Messiah needs to be qualified in various ways. Talking about salvation requires the same qualifications. One may agree with the author that, within a particular religious tradition and when talking to a specific audience that shares that religious tradition, everything may make sense, and that the theological claims are understood and accepted without question. However, scholarship is prudent and humble; it involves painstakingly searching for answers and probing various truths, as opposed to evangelism or preaching. This is a different game. I hope we can both agree on that.

BIRD: "MESSIANIC ESCHATOLOGY AND SUPERSESSIONISM"

The thesis of Bird's essay is that "Paul indeed thinks of his gentile assemblies as belonging to 'Israel,' as they are grafted into God's covenant people when they are grafted into Israel's Messiah" (45). As presented, the thesis is clear. It does not announce any schema of supersessionism, despite the essay's title ("Paul's Messianic Eschatology and Supersessionism"). It is confusing to me that the stated aim is different from the one implied in the essay's thesis. Bird's assertion that "in this essay, I intend to exposit the contours of Paul's supersessionism in light of modern scholarship" (47) expresses an altogether divergent goal.

From the introduction, one may admire Bird's tentative approach to what Paul believed, or what he thinks Paul believed, or what he thought Paul was doing. Bird states, "Paul's 'messianic eschatology' seems to necessitate some variety of supersessionism, with Paul believing that Israel is redefined around the Messiah and the Spirit" (46). I understand the hesitation, but I wonder whether Paul's "messianic eschatology" really necessitated a kind of supersesionism. Following the previous quoted sentence, Bird states, "This is an inescapable inference, given that Paul believed that he was right and his fellow Jews were wrong" (46). So what? We all have hope we are always right and that our neighbors, friends, family members, spouses, or colleagues are permanently wrong, especially when they do not arrive at the same conclusions as ours. But so what? This does not mean we are always right and they are always wrong. The same logic applies to Paul. He was actively theologizing according to what he believed was the special revelation he received from Christ. The fact he believed that he was right and his fellow Jews were wrong on some specific issues does not make him right and they wrong. As scholars, we can appreciate how Paul develops certain deeply held convictions about God, Torah, and the place of non-Jews in God's covenantal blessings in light of his Damascus-road experience. We can try to understand the logic of what he was doing without making the leap to state he was right and all others within his religious tradition who have thought or continue to think differently from Paul about God, the place of Torah, and the place of non-Jews within Jewish tradition are wrong.

Bird's actual development of supersessionism in scholarship is sketchy and does not engage any biblical scholars presenting a challenge to his view on the topic. Those mentioned in the footnotes (Scot McKnight, Doug Campbell, N. T. Wright, and Bruce Marshall) are on his side, with minor nuances, and the other scholars mentioned are Christian systematic theologians (Douglas Harink, R. Kendall Soulen, Steven D. Aguzzi) and one Jewish theologian and ethicist (David Novak). It would have been helpful to engage the arguments of those from the other side of the scholarly divide on the issue, especially under his subheading of "supersessionism in scholarship."

Furthermore, it would have been helpful for Bird to clarify what he means by "the aversion to supersessionism" (48) experienced by many as symptomatic of a deeper sociological malaise than about the designation itself. As someone with a keen interest in the sociology of religion, I would have been eager to learn more about the sociology of religious scholarship, had this point been developed. For Bird, "supersessionism, then, sadly amounts to nothing more than a mode of scholarly, in-house, deviant-labeling" (49). Again, it would have been useful to develop this thought. But how does he know that?

Later in the essay, Bird shows he understands the traumatic legacy of Christian supersessionism, but he maintains that one should not equate any talk about the topic with a crude use of the term. It is, according to him, "not a single thing"; it is, rather, "a family of views about Paul and the Jews that some scholars believe requires decontamination from their discourse" (49). Yet he does not hesitate to refer to the problematic, probably un-Pauline 1 Thessalonians 2:14–16 text, although he qualifies it as a passage that is "jarring and make[s] us cringe" (49).

I agree with Bird that "what Paul said is one thing; what we choose to do with it is quite another" (49), but I would also add that we need to remember that Paul was of his time and place. He spoke and acted in a context that was different from ours. We should bear the burdens of our own time and space, instead of reverting sometimes too eagerly and too readily to what Paul said about various issues in his own time and context.

INEVITABLE SUPERSESSIONISM?

With examples from some Jewish texts, Bird moves on to advance the argument that supersessionism is inevitable. The logic goes as follows: since Paul is Jewish, we need to understand him within Judaism, and because the discourse regarding supersessionism is entirely Jewish, it follows that Paul is participating in a very Jewish tradition by presenting his arguments in a supersessionistic way. I am simply paraphrasing Bird: "Paul's supersessionism is inherited from his Jewish framework, worked out in a messianic matrix which itself draws heavily on the Jewish scriptures and was asserted in the fractious socio-religious context of the eastern Mediterranean diaspora" (53–54).

Bird invokes a fierce honesty in his appeal to accept Paul's supersessionism: "To be brutally honest, supersessionism is simply unavoidable if we are engaging in a close and contextual reading of Paul within Judaism" (54). But, to be really honest, this is not Paul's language. Continuation, yes, but not another group supplanting or dislodging the other. Paul has never referred to "Christians"—or, God forbid, to "Christianity"—superseding "Judaism." Paul does not talk of non-Jews becoming members of Judaism. If we want to understand Paul within his own context, we cannot impose on him languages and concepts he does not use. These remarks are in response to what Bird says in the following excerpt:

> When one expounds Paul's penetrating statements about Torah and sin [sic., it should be Sin, because Paul understands 'Sin' as a power], salvation of [sic., it should be "in"] Christ and not the Torah, Jewish antagonism towards the gospel [too broad and undefined], and the place of gentiles as members God's people [sic., add "of" before "God"] without becoming proselytes to Judaism [really? define what you mean by "Judaism" since Paul never refers to it as a belief system but as the ways in which he had devoted his life to Judaean customs and Judaean law before his encounter with Christ], then, supersessionism is simply inescapable. (54)

SUPERIOR VIEW?

Bird reinforces his argument for supersessionism because, in his opinion, "Paul believed in the superiority of his inclusive view over the exclusive view of his compatriots" (56). There are two problems with this statement: first, Paul's supposedly superior belief; second, Paul as being unlike his compatriots. *Believing* one's position is right or superior to that of another does not *make* such position right or superior. The binaries of right versus wrong and superior versus inferior are problematic on so many levels that I will not enter into the issues here.

The second slippery slope in the argument is portraying Paul as Jewish, but as one unlike his Jewish compatriots. For Bird, Paul was an inclusive Jew, whereas his compatriots were exclusive Jews. Paul was the hero who stood up for inclusivity with the non-Jews, whereas his villainous Jewish kinfolks were rigid exclusivists. I wish a much more nuanced understanding of Paul and his fellow Judaeans had been developed within this very informative essay. Much has been written already with regard to the dangers of characterizing Paul as so unlike his fellow Jews, and some of these nuances should have informed Bird's thinking.[1]

Before looking at the last few pages and conclusion of my colleague's paper, I am frankly wondering what's at stake in this presentation. Instead of presenting Paul as *sui generis*, and in place of putting so much energy on supersessionism—which is a contested and problematic label imposed on Paul, notwithstanding Bird's plea to consider it in much more flexible or varied ways—would it be possible to present Paul in a different light? Would it be at all a worthy scholarly project to try to understand Paul and what he believed about what was communicated or revealed to him about his ancestral traditions, and how non-Jews could be included in that tradition, without resorting to supersessionism?

FINAL EXPOSITION

I have a few questions for purposes of clarification. Bird mentions that, according to 1 Corinthians 7:19; and Galatians 5:6 and 6:15, circumcision is nullified. For which group? Jews? Non-Jews? Christ-believing Jews? Christ-believing non-Jews?

Bird also notes that Paul says Israel has experienced "rejection" (Rom 11:28), but God has "not rejected his people" (11:1–2). Bird then softens these two clearly contradictory statements with the coy admission that "the tension here is real" (60). This is more than mere

---

1. See in particular William Arnal, "The Collection and Synthesis of 'Tradition' and the Second-Century Invention of Christianity," *MTSR* 23 (2011): 193–215.

tension. It cannot be both. Any other of my religious studies colleagues in my department would look at these statements and say:
"These are not the same." Why defend Paul?

In addition, when Bird advances that "Israel can and will be saved,"
he clarifies that this salvation depends on faith in Christ: "if they do
not persist in unbelief (Rom 11:23)" (60). Paul's view is accepted
without question. This is a particular Christian perspective—that is,
it is a particular construction of Christianity developed from Paul.
However, does that render the statement gospel truth?

At "the heart of Christianity," in Bird's understanding, is "the singularity of salvation in Christ and the giving of the Spirit to non-
Jews..., the secondment of the Torah in the service of sin and death,
the inability of the Torah to save and define God's people, Israel's
stumbling for its rejection of Christ and clinging to the Torah for
righteousness, and the expansion of Israel to include non-Jews" (62).
One may ponder what constitutes "the heart" of this religious tradition that came to be known as Christianity. I dare say that many of
today's Christians, especially those living in the global South, in the
lost places of the globe, and in the impoverished places of the planet
would probably not identify these formulaic and fine points as "the
heart" of their faith. Many of those who are observing Christians
living in their midst would probably not identify these points as the
heart of what makes these people Christians either.

Finally, one may ask whether the conclusion Bird reaches is coherent or genuine with respect to the place of those who are not Jews
and not Christians. His recommendation is that Christians should
not denigrate "those who share in the flesh and family of the Jewish
Messiah" (64), because Jesus is Jewish and salvation cannot be conceived outside the Jewish matrix from which it originates. Is this theological conclusion not masquerading as genuinely caring for Jews
when at the bottom of the reasoning is the proviso that unless you
become like us, Christians, with faith in Christ—sorry, no salvation
for you?

WITHERINGTON: "PAUL, GALATIANS, AND SUPERSESSIONISM"

Ben Witherington's essay sets out to show how the Paul-within-Judaism paradigm cannot fit with Paul's argument in his letter to the Galatians. Witherington states at the outset, "it is not too much to say that the Paul-within-Judaism point of view has had a very hard time fitting Galatians into their larger argument that Paul lived out his religious life within his native Judaism, and was not the creator of the 'partings of the ways' between early Judaism and the Christ movement" (66). Furthermore, Witherington advances that if Paul were still within Judaism he would not have said he "is prepared to say he counts his old identity and way of life as *skubala*" (68). To be clear, in Philippians 3:8, Paul states that he considers everything a loss in comparison or with respect to the superior value of knowing Christ. For Christ, he has suffered the loss of all things, and what he has lost he considers *skubala*, that he might gain Christ. Paul's logic seems to be readily apparent here, not that the things in themselves are *skubala*, but that he considers all of his ethnic pedigree (Phil 3:4–5) a loss in comparison or with respect to the superior value of knowing Christ. For Paul, anything that would push him to consider himself superior to others (non-Jews), based on his Jewish heritage, he regards as *skubala*, so that he may gain Christ. The point of all this is that Paul did not say his (old) identity and way of life are *skubala* in a non-qualified way.

Following that misunderstanding, Witherington advances two other problematic statements—first, that Paul's reference to *skubala* makes it hard to see him as "remaining in the Judaism he was formerly a part of" (68). Paul, in effect, moved from one form of serving God within his ancestral traditions to other ways of serving God within his ancestral traditions, albeit in new/redefined/readjusted ways in Paul's mind and theological convictions. The second statement that needed to be clearly explained is that Paul "is no longer chiefly identifying himself in terms of his ethnic Jewishness, but will adopt Jewish praxis for missional reasons" (68). Was Paul somehow identifying himself in terms of his ethnic Jewishness but not "chiefly" doing so? Did Paul cease to be Jewish? Was he simply performing Jewishness when with Jews and performing as a non-Jew when with non-Jews to gain converts? The answer to these questions is obviously no. Paul was deeply formed and moved by his ancestral traditions. His Jewish heritage profoundly shaped his theology. In fact, Witherington abounds in this direction as well, stating that "Paul places his whole Jewish heritage at the service of, and subordinate to, the ultimate value of 'knowing Christ' (Phil 3:4–11)" (70). But why then come with the assertion that "if Torah-observance would destroy the unity among believers or would form a barrier to gentile access to Christ, it would be better for Jews like Peter and Paul to live 'in a gentile fashion' (Gal 2:11–14)" (70). That's trying to jump on various planes at once. In the case of Galatians 2, the issue is not Torah-observance as a threat to the unity among believers. The inclusion of Peter and Paul into the discussion is not clear, especially if they are thus presented—that is, separated from the particular issue of Galatians 2 as reported by Paul.

ISSUES OF ANACHRONISM

Witherington rightly mentions issues of anachronism in the debate of interest. For example, he laments how modern suggestions creep into the discussion without actual evidence from antiquity. He is cautious to flag how a term like "supersessionism," the central element of this volume, is anachronistic. For this, I applaud him. However, Witherington could have been equally careful not to use a problematic term such as "religion" when he states, for example, that there were "considerable variety of praxis as well as beliefs in that religion" (70) when he wanted to refer to the diversity that existed in the Jewish ancestral tradition(s) of Paul's time. He also could be more careful with his use of the term "Christian" to talk about early Christ-followers or "Old Testament" to refer to Jewish scripture.[2] For Paul,

---

2. References to "church" for the gathering of early Christ-groups is also anachronistic. See Jennifer Eyl, "Semantic Voids, New Testament Translation, and Anachronism: The Case of Paul's Use of *Ekklēsia*," *MTSR* 26 (2014): 4–5.

his Bible was the Jewish scripture. Witherington admits that much when he states that, to Paul, "Christ is seen as part of the divine identity to whom his converts could now pray *marana tha*—'come O Lord'— knowing full well that Jews pray only to the God of the Bible" (78).

EXEGETICAL MISREADINGS

Witherington delves into the incident at Antioch, as recounted by Paul in Galatians 2. And this is an important point: whatever happened at Antioch, it is reported through Paul's lenses and with his rhetorical *tour de force* to advance his own theological agenda. In reading such a report, scholars need to be more careful not to accept that Peter was indeed acting as a hypocrite. Paul's theological conclusions are his. They may make sense to him, but that does not mean they do indeed make sense to everyone. In fact, many Jews and non-Jews in the past, as well in the present, do not see or understand many of Paul's conclusions. Few Pauline scholars would be so bold as to state they understand him clearly. Paul is extremely interesting as a thinker, pastor, apostle to the *ethne*, as he was engaging and actively theologizing in light of his calling. However, one should be cautious in stating bluntly, without qualification, that "the Pauline gospel involved an inherent critique of the majority of Jews for not recognizing their own Messiah and for failing to realize that the eschatological time had come for one and all to embrace a new covenant inaugurated by Christ's death and resurrection" (72).

It is not clear to me what Witherington means by the following excerpt: "In short, though the Mosaic law had an important function in its day and time, its day and time had come and gone, and that same law (as well as the 'time'; 4:4) had been fulfilled by what Christ brought to God's people" (74). I find the clause "its day and time had come and gone" rather unclear. Does it presuppose that Torah had come and gone for Jews? Should they forget or move completely away from the God-given gift of Torah to them once or if they become a Christ-follower?

Is Paul advocating for the Christ-followers in Galatians, regardless of whether they are Jewish or not, to no longer keep Torah? Witherington surmises that what Paul is "rejecting is the necessity of keeping the Mosaic law if one is a Christian" (75). This is completely different from the argument Paul is making in Galatians. He does not want the Galatians (should I specify they were non-Jews?) to think they are missing something in their walk with God by not embracing specific Jewish rituals (circumcision, dietary rules, keeping of the Sabbath) and by not incorporating elements from their native and social cultural views on God ("elemental spirits," 4:9). In the gospel of Christ he preached to them, Paul argues, they have everything. The Galatians need not go and try to become Jewish, because they simply are not Jewish. In making this point, Paul certainly exaggerates his rhetoric in a cringe-worthy manner with regard to Torah, circumcision, Sabbath, and even the place of Jerusalem (split in two in his arguments). These are rhetorical constructions with specific theological aims in a specific context and argument. However, in the midst of all his rhetorical bravado, Paul does not say that if one is a Christian one should not keep the Mosaic law, as if he were addressing Jews.

Furthermore, what does Witherington mean by "the time"? Which time? Is he referring to a redefined people (Jews and non-Jews) when he mentions that the time had been fulfilled by what Christ has done to (or on behalf of) God's people? It seems that this is what Witherington understands when he states that "the people of God has become Jew and gentile united in the Jewish Messiah" (74). I certainly appreciate Witherington's acknowledgment that Paul's debate in Galatians 4 is an intramural discussion between Paul and other Jewish Christ-followers with regard to how non-Jews may be part of the overall Abrahamic blessings, but why even nod to the ridiculous view that Paul "certainly does not see Christianity as replacing Judaism" (74)? Moreover, why keep the anachronistic and problematic term "Christianity" in the following sentence: "Paul is not defending gentile Christianity at the expense of Jewish Christianity" (75)?

A subsequent question worth pondering is whether Paul still viewed himself as a Jewish person or not. Witherington answers both ways—no and yes.

> *No:* "He is no longer chiefly identifying himself in terms of his ethnic Jewishness, but will adopt Jewish praxis for missional reasons, so he might win some Jews to Christ" (68).

> *Yes:* "We may suspect that since Paul still views himself and other Christians as Jews, then 'all those who follow this rule' would of course include himself, whom he is perhaps distinguishing from the as-of-yet-not-saved 'Israel of God'" (76).

We cannot have it both ways. Witherington needs to provide a clear answer to the question. My own understanding is that Paul continued to see himself as belonging to his ancestral tradition. He does not give the impression of being one who has any qualm in observing and participating in cultural and religious elements of his heritage, especially when he is among his own kinship group.

It is true, as Witherington notes, that Romans 9–11 shows clearly how Paul agonizes over the fate of his people who have not accepted his Messiah. Certainly, in Romans 11:26 Paul states, "all Israel will be saved," but it is not clear to me from reading the whole context of the text that Paul is referring to a mass Jewish conversion to Christ in the eschaton. Nonetheless, this is Witherington's reading:

> He says that he would even be prepared to be cut off from Christ if they could be saved, and in the end, at Romans 11:26 he foresees an eschatological miracle of conversion of Jews to Christ. ... One must bear in mind that it is a largely gentile audience Paul is addressing in Romans, including Romans 9–11. But who he talks *about* in Romans 9–11 is both gentiles and Jews and their future in Christ. (76)

The question is: On what exegetical basis does Witherington make such a distinction and logical leap? A reader may be forgiven for feeling a bit confused, not only about this reading of Romans 9–11 but also about the argumentative space Romans 9–11 occupies in an essay on Paul, Galatians, and supersessionism. Thus, when Witherington nods quickly to Galatians 6:16 to show a supposed link to Romans' reference to "non-Christian Jews," one is left scratching one's head trying to understand the correlation.

What I understand Paul to be saying in Romans 11:25–26 (too briefly, I admit) is that while part of Israel is hardened in the present time, salvation has come to the *ethne*. However, Israel's current and negative position (that is, its partial hardening) is only temporary. When the "fullness of the *ethne* has come in" then the eschatological age will be ushered in with the salvation of all Israel.

WAS PAUL A SUPERSESSIONIST?

This question informs the last section of Witherington's essay. But, surprise! Witherington admits, "In many ways, the modern discussion of both early Judaism and early Christianity has suffered from the use of anachronistic terms like 'supersessionism,' a term Paul would not recognize" (77). Exactly! I continue to be surprised: "Neither would he recognize the notion that the assembly of God in Christ, composed of Jew and gentile alike, should simply be called Israel" (77). Is that not what Witherington articulated earlier? He goes back once again to Romans 11:26: "all Israel" (adding what is not in the text) "would be saved by grace through faith in Jesus" (77). Yet he leaves room for a sovereign God who "can still have mercy even on those who have rejected Jesus of Nazareth, and Paul believes he will do so at the parousia" (78). So on that we are clear; God can save all Israel, without the specificity of faith in Christ. It is not clear why "Paul believes he will do so at the parousia." For Witherington, "there is no contradiction here, for Paul believes that God has a plan, however mysterious, for Israel and the assembly of God composed of Jew and gentile to be one people of God in the end" (79). Certainly, Paul wishes, dreams, believes that God has a mysterious plan and that, in the end, "all Israel will be saved." He does not say how. It is, remember, a mystery. In the meantime, we can try to understand what Paul said and what he hoped and dreamed for. We may also endeavor to live our lives in our own time and space as best we are able, according to the gifts, talents, and abilities we have, and to make a difference in the lives of all—Jews and non-Jews—without being utterly preoccupied to know whether Paul was a supersessionist or not.

I thank my colleagues for their essays, and especially Michael Bird, for inviting me to provide this critical response.

CONCLUDING REFLECTIONS

SCOT MCKNIGHT

I have never once enjoyed this conversation—not because the intellectual challenges are not formidable and the exegeses demanding, but because there is nothing enjoyable about discussing what one thinks another person has wrong. But no matter how much we disagree, I want to add that the undeniable implication of so much of the supersessionist mentality has been a vicious, sinful, sickening racism. I deplore it, and what I most fear is that any firm disagreement between Christians and Jews, or between Messianic Jewish Christians and gentile believers, might be put to use in a racist manner. The racial implications of some forms of supersessionism have been exposed by the brilliant scholars Willie James Jennings and J. Kameron Carter. I applaud their efforts, as well, in showing how racist supersessionism has created various forms of colonialism and degradation of non-whites. I believe tolerance of difference denounces these bastard forms of disagreement.[1]

When I read what Lynn Cohick said to open her essay—"rarely have I felt so uncomfortable with my Christian heritage" (83)—I said, "Yes, that's it." As a panelist at an academic conference I felt the same, and yet there was a need for someone to take a stand on what I think is a crucial factor. Not only do the post-supersessionists recreate in some

---

1. Willie James Jennings, *The Christian Imagination: Theology and the Origins of Race* (New Haven: Yale University Press, 2011); J. Kameron Carter, *Race: A Theological Account* (New York: Oxford University Press, 2008).

ways the Galatian situation itself, but one has to consider whether the apostle Paul thought his Jewish friends and family were in need of hearing and responding to the gospel. It is, then, no light matter to ask if Jesus was indeed the Jewish Messiah. An affirmative answer to such a question has innumerable implications.

David Rudolph, who refuses to answer my questions, wants instead for Mike Bird and me to answer his two questions—and his questions actually shed light on this discussion, because they imply a rather narrow theory of what supersessionism means. Here are his questions (from pages 103, 106), followed by my answers:

Are nonmessianic Jews members of God's covenanted people?

And, if so, do they as a people have a unique covenantal call-ing that distinguishes their calling from that of every other society or nation?

To number one: Yes, they are members of God's covenant with Israel—always have been and always will be. Paul's words in Romans 11:28–29 could not be clearer: "As regards the gospel they are ene-mies of God for your sake; but as regards election they are beloved, for the sake of their ancestors; for the gifts and the calling of God are irrevocable."[2] Peters says something valuable in this regard, though her last clause has content that will come up again and again in this concluding reflection:

The image of the eternal plant is not as negative as it appears at first glance, as it also suggests that even in Paul's day the church resorted to a fusion of Judaism and Christianity that was more effective as a tactic than a strategy. This agrees with the 2015 Roman Catholic reading of Romans whereby the Jewish cove-nant cannot be revoked, whether or not Jews follow Christ. (134)

---

2. Scripture quotations in the conclusion are the author's translation.

But Rudolph's "members of God's covenanted people" begs the question of what "covenanted" means for Rudolph.

To number two: Yes, they have a distinct calling, which they have exercised and can still continue to exercise. They are to embody God's covenant with Israel both personally and corporately, and they are to call people to an eschatological faith that comes to expression in Jesus of Nazareth as Messiah.

I asked him if all Jews need to believe in Jesus to be saved. I await his answer. Peters answers my question with a solid no!

> Jews and Catholics believe in the same God of Israel, but the way they envision God giving covenants differs radically. Simply putting Paul within Judaism will be a stopgap measure for casual anti-Semitism on the part of churchgoers, but it ignores the real disagreements between Paul and the synagogues in which he debated. There was and is some supersession between forms of Judaism and Christianity, but that Catholics need not proselytize Jews means that Jews are saved with only the Jewish covenant. Although Paul, a former Pharisee, couldn't resist engaging in dialogue with his former Jewish colleagues, the Roman Catholic Church must definitely not pressure Jews into following Christ. Jews have salvation on their own terms. (145)

I wonder whether she thinks Paul would agree. He wouldn't. His life makes no sense if that were his mission theology.

Bird has the nettle in his hand in recognizing how the term "supersessionism" is used today. He writes, "But if supersessionism can cover a multitude of perspectives about the church vis-à-vis the Jews—i.e., antiquation, representation, replacement, supplement, succession, superiority, superordination, etc.—then it is so broad as to be baseless as a criticism" (48). He adds:

> Supersessionism, then, sadly amounts to nothing more than a mode of scholarly in-house deviant-labeling against any

interpreter daring to articulate a perspective on Paul that is not sufficiently conducive to some preferred vision of inter-faith relationships. (49)

The term "supersessionism" is a powerful piece of rhetoric—a rhetoric unfortunately on display in Ronald Charles's response with not a little whiff of virtue-signaling. Bird digs his heels in gently by saying supersessionism is the way of Jewish sectarianism; it is inevitable and inescapable. Yet I ask myself over and over if it is eradicable and inescapable, because I know the term is at times irresponsible. What is inexcusable is anti-Semitism, intolerant disagreements with Judaism, and relationships that are so fractured that the gospel itself about Jesus as Messiah is inaudible and inexpressible. The history of Christian anti-Semitism and even the history of polemics between Christianity and Judaism are immeasurably damaging. But Rudolph offers a reminder I want to keep in front of me always:

> While supersessionism has different meanings today and the term can be misused, there is a place for recognizing what it originally meant before it sprouted so many variations. In his monograph *Aquinas on Israel and the Church*, Matthew Tapie surveys the history of the term and articulates the heart of its meaning in Christianity's traditional theology of the Jewish people. He concludes, "*Supersessionism is the Christian claim that with the advent of Christ, Jewish law is fulfilled and obsolete, with the result that God replaces Israel with the Church.*" (127; italics original)

Yet the question of salvation forces the substance behind the term into play and this leads me to say that I prefer to ignore this term when I can by speaking instead of *expansionism*. That is, the people of God expands to include gentiles on the basis of faith in Jesus as Messiah. Israel is not replaced but expanded—but that expansion, the apostle Paul says, occurs in Christ and through Christ in what Paul calls the "mystery," and in Romans 11 he announces that at some future date "all" Israel will be saved. In that most crucial moment of Paul's explanation of himself, in Galatians, we can find how he thinks about the very question we are asking today. The heart of his argument is found in Galatians 3:16–29, which I will include here so as to make commenting easier:

> Now the promises were made to Abraham and to his offspring; it does not say, "And to offsprings," as of many; but it says, "And to your offspring," that is, to one person, who is Christ. My point is this: the law, which came four hundred thirty years later, does not annul a covenant previously ratified by God, so as to nullify the promise. For if the inheritance comes from the law, it no longer comes from the promise; but God granted it to Abraham through the promise.
>
> Why then the law? It was added because of transgressions, until the offspring would come to whom the promise had been made; and it was ordained through angels by a mediator. Now a mediator involves more than one party; but God is one.
>
> Is the law then opposed to the promises of God? Certainly not! For if a law had been given that could make alive, then righteousness would indeed come through the law. But the scripture has imprisoned all things under the power of sin, so that what was promised through faith in Jesus Christ might be given to those who believe.
>
> Now before faith came, we were imprisoned and guarded under the law until faith would be revealed. Therefore the law was our disciplinarian until Christ came, so that we might be justified by faith. But now that faith has come, we are no longer subject to a disciplinarian, for in Christ Jesus you are all children of God through faith. As many of you as were baptized into Christ have clothed yourselves with Christ. There is no longer Jew or Greek, there is no longer slave or free, there is no longer male and female; for all of you are one in Christ Jesus.

And if you belong to Christ, then you are Abraham's offspring, heirs according to the promise.

The charge by some—and I think they are Jewish believers (and I have respect for, but disagree with, those who think these are gentiles who have become zealous for the Torah for all believers)—is that Paul is getting loose with Torah. One point he makes then is that the covenant is about promise and not Torah, so the covenant has priority. It trumps Torah. So why was the Torah added some four hundred years later? His answer is direct: "because of transgressions" (v. 19).

The next words of verse 19 have shaped my mind: "until the offspring" comes, who is Christ. This puts a *terminus ad quem* on the Torah. From Moses to Christ the Torah obtained; with Christ something changed—which statement provokes Paul's opponents in Galatia into asking (in an almost Lutheran fashion) whether the Torah is not then opposed to the "promises of God" (the covenant with Abraham). The Torah, Paul says, never was given to give life or righteousness. In fact, the Torah's job—from Moses until Christ, remember—was to imprison "all things under the power of sin" (v. 22). This happened to provoke faith in Christ Jesus.

Paul has a salvation-historical timeline:

Abraham → Moses/Law → Christ/Faith/Spirit

Until Christ or faith came, "we" were imprisoned. (The terms "I" and "we" in Galatians—and for that matter Romans—have been parsed in all ways, but one cannot parse them cleanly enough to know whether or not "they" refers consistently to one ethnic group.) The only persons imprisoned from Moses to Christ under Torah were Israel. The Torah was a "disciplinarian" (v. 24) that God used "until faith would be revealed" (v. 23).

The momentous words are "now that faith has come, we are *no longer subject to a disciplinarian*" (v. 25). To back up one chapter in Galatians, this is what Paul means by dying to the Torah through the Torah in 2:15–21. It is why he says that wall must not be rebuilt in the same passage. Unity has new life. We are all now in Christ—those who are baptized into Christ by faith—and there is "no longer Jew or Greek, ... slave or free, ... male and female" (3:28). This does not erase distinctions—and the post-supersessionists are so helpful in keeping this clear—but it provides a context in which they are transcended in Christ without diminishing the distinctions. There is no reason for anyone to think Messianic Jews need to surrender Torah-observance, so long as it does not break fellowship, and there is no reason for gentile believers to denounce Messianic Jews for observing Torah. Kosher food laws are subject to missional living (1 Cor 9:19–23). I would gladly surrender bacon if it offends my brother or sister, but only so long as no-bacon is not required of all believers.

But it is passages like Galatians 2–3 that lead Witherington to these not-so-subtle but also not uncharitable remarks:

> The attempt to tame Paul and make him still fit into early Jewish shoes of an ordinary sort only with a messianic logo on them rather than a Nike swoosh was rightly warned against by two of the best Jewish scholars in our field—both A. Segal and D. Boyarin. Paul was indeed a radical Jew, one who would not and will not be neatly fit even into the surprising diversity of early Judaism as it existed before Christ. He believed of course that the Hebrew Bible was the Word of God, that Jesus was both the Jewish messiah and the savior of gentiles, he believed the Scriptures were being fulfilled and the eschatological dreams of Isaiah and others were coming to pass. He also believed that God had given Israel covenants plural (Rom. 9.1–5) not just a single covenant renewed again and again. (66)

The two-covenant approaches of some, which is a version of either pluralism or universalism, lurks in the discussion, and I called attention to it. Charles's critique of my particularism carries with it the irony of his own particularism used against someone for having a particularism. Witherington will have none of the lurking pluralism:

In many ways, the modern discussion of both early Judaism
and early Christianity has suffered from the use of anachronistic terms like "supersessionism," a term Paul would not recognize. Neither would he recognize the notion that the assembly
of God in Christ, composed of Jew and gentile alike, should
simply be called Israel, or seen as the sequel or replacement
for Israel. No, for Paul, Israel, still had a future, but that future
was "in Christ."

Nor would Paul recognize the modern two-track model of salvation—Jews through being Torah true, gentiles through Jesus.
Without question, for Paul, Jesus is both the messiah for Israel
and the Savior of the gentile world. (77)

Witherington time and time has come in his writings and does
come in this book to the conclusion of Bird, Cohick, and me: If Jesus
is the Messiah, what then? As Cohick says it,

My understanding of the term "supersessionism" in Paul's letters differs little from the three authors' positions stated here.
I concur that supersessionism understood as replacement theology is not found in Paul's letters; however, supersessionism
understood as a conviction that Jesus Christ is the fulfillment
of the biblical promises of redemption for all people is consistent with Paul's gospel message. Rather than a robust rebuttal,
I offer affirming applause. (84)

In a recent study, Douglas Farrow asks if faithful Jews ought to
believe in Jesus and thus if they are to be gospeled. His answer is to
look at the parousia, and he contends that in the New Testament a
parousia-shaped mission theology urges us to think that Jews will not
only turn to Jesus then but are to be called to Jesus now.[3] Again, the
question remains: What if Jesus is the Messiah?

---

3. Douglas Farrow, "*Blessed is he who comes in the name of the LORD*: Jews and
the Parousia of Jesus," *Communio* 45.3–4 (2018). .

The "What if?" question has been asked over and over by N. T. Wright, who comes in for particularly heated treatment by Rudolph, and Wright returns to this again in his commentary on Galatians. The answer is "yes" and the implication is unity. Wright, again:

> In particular—and I know how difficult and contentious this is—I think Paul would be deeply saddened to think that those who now call themselves "messianic Jews" might feel obliged to see themselves as different from gentile Christians. I understand how that situation has come about, and I honor those who have struggled to find a genuine integrity amid horrible pressures, tragic history, and deep prejudice. But just as the danger for gentile Christians, still, is to regard the Jewish people either as a strange anachronism or, in reaction to that, as a kind of beacon of hope to the world—with all the ramifications of this in popular American eschatology! —so the danger for Jewish Christians is to retreat, like the rival teachers in Galatia, into a world where the Messiah has not yet won the victory, where the Torah still rules supreme. I know these are huge issues, but it would be wrong not at least to touch on them.[4]

Wright digs a deeper trench here than I would, but his spade is in the right spot. The issue is unity, and a unity achievable only in union with Christ.

I conclude with Bird's conclusion, because it brings the whole book to its defining point and makes me think the only way forward is to affirm one another, to affirm our differences, and to affirm one another yet again:

> Paul's "messianic eschatology" seems to necessitate some variety of supersessionism, with Paul believing that Israel is

---

4. N. T. Wright, *Galatians*, Commentaries for Christian Formation (Grand Rapids: Eerdmans, 2021), 246.

redefined around the Messiah and the Spirit. This is an inescapable inference given that Paul believed that he was right
and his fellow Jews were wrong. They were wrong about Jesus
as the crucified and exalted Lord, wrong about whether the
end was here and nigh, wrong about how gentiles could be
reconciled to God, wrong to oppose his message and ministry among Jews and gentiles, and wrong about the lines that
separated the faithful from the apostate in this new age. Paul
is supersessionist in the sense that he is sectarian; he believes
that his view of God, gentiles, Messiah, the end, covenant fidelity, and community boundaries should be the norm in Jewish
communities. (46-47)

However, the mere mention of supersessionism causes umbrage
and alarm. Have we now given succour to Chrysostom and his Jew-
hating tirades that God has renounced the Jews and replaced them
with Christians? Personally, I hope not! But we cannot avoid the inevitability of supersessionism in Paul, and we do best to offer a refined
analysis of it and then make an informed response to it.

We cannot help but read Paul—as well as Matthew, John, Ignatius,
Chrysostom, Luther, and Barth—except in light of the horror of Shoah,
and we must read responsibly. We can ask: Would Paul have written
what he did in Romans 9–11, Galatians 4, and 1 Thessalonians 2:14–16
if he knew the history we knew? Should we follow Paul, given that we
know where this all led? Should we not burn and bury every instance
of supersessionism for its christological dogmatism? The challenge for
Christians is to simultaneously affirm the *solus Christus* (Christ alone
is Savior) of their confession and the proposition that *extra Israel nulla
salus* (outside of Israel there is no salvation) without denigrating those
who share in the flesh and family of the Jewish Messiah.

SUBJECT & AUTHOR INDEX

SCRIPTURE & EXTRABIBLICAL SOURCES INDEX

MISCELLANEOUS SOURCES